Live

Inspired Now

Praise For *Live Inspired Now*:

"*Live Inspired Now: A Field Guide for Happiness* is an easy-to-read, fun-filled yet touching journey to inspiration and the realization that happiness is right there waiting for every single one of us!"

> —Betsy Chasse, author of *Tipping Sacred Cows* and *What the Bleep Do We Know?!*

"Heather's perspective is absolutely refreshing. She reminds us what is really important and how easy it is to be happy. She reminds us that it is always our choice and that we are more powerful than we realize or give ourselves credit for. I laughed and cried while reading her truly heartfelt, honest, and sometimes vulnerable stories. Don't waste time; read it and start living inspired now!"
—Peg Haust-Arliss, LCSW-R

"*Live Inspired Now: A Field Guide for Happiness* is a great expression of how positive attitude, love, compassion, and kindness should be implemented daily in our lives so we can live the best life we can while we are here. No matter what challenges life throws at you, it doesn't have any meaning until you give it one. After reading this, you will see how choosing happiness and living an inspired life is the only way to live."
—Jodi Brichta-Coyne, mother of two

Live Inspired Now

A Field Guide For Happiness

HEATHER PARIS

BALBOA
PRESS

A DIVISION OF HAY HOUSE

Balboa Press books may be ordered through booksellers or by contacting:

Balboa Press
A Division of Hay House
1663 Liberty Drive
Bloomington, IN 47403
www.balboapress.com
1 (877) 407-4847

Printed in the United States of America.

ISBN: 978-1-4525-8289-4 (sc)
ISBN: 978-1-4525-8291-7 (hc)
ISBN: 978-1-4525-8290-0 (e)

Library of Congress Control Number: 2013919793

Balboa Press rev. date: 10/30/2013

For Thad, my inspiration.

TABLE OF CONTENTS

INTRODUCTION

Four marriages, three kids, thirty-some addresses, a great deal of laughter, too many tears, and an absolute lust for life that always kept me inspired: This is how my story begins.

I am a mother to six children, three that are my own and three that I am happy to call my own. I am married to the best husband on the entire planet. He loves me, supports me and accepts me just as I am. He is my soul mate, my best friend, my life partner, my co-pilot and my all around favorite person. And, I am fortunate to be all of these things to Thad, in return.

Before you learn how I met him, I want to give you the short version of my life before Thad. I think it will make it easier for you to understand the stories I choose to share with you. So, here it goes…

I have always been the type of person that would bring home stray animals and friends. I love people and have a natural tendency to want to take care of them. This is likely the reason I married three different men that I thought needed me. My daughter Madison's father is an alcoholic. I thought I could fix him. Harry's father has bi-polar disorder and I thought I could help him. And Carrie's dad was being taken advantage of by an old flame and I wanted to help free him. What can I say? I thought I could help, fix, change, free and/or save them and I liked the feeling of importance it gave me. I know now that trying to save someone is not the way to a good relationship.

We all get along just fine - now. That wasn't the case early on but through my own personal evolution I've learned plenty about happiness and how it to find it. Through my deep desire to feel needed and to feel like I was making a difference, I discovered the way to freedom and fulfillment was not in trying to save people, but in working on being a positive force and example for everyone. Whether we decide to save ourselves from a tormented life, or to live in turmoil, is a choice we make on our own.

After three failed marriages, I decided to dedicate my life to serving others and gave up on finding love for myself. However, love always prevails. Just when I had given up on finding love, I met my soul mate, Thad. I believe the stars truly aligned to bring us together. We had both been in abusive relationships and married to people with addictive behaviors. We each had three children (all of which are the same ages) and we shared a passion for helping and serving others. Once we realized we were meant to be together, we didn't hold back. Today we are very happily married and love every magic moment of our life together. I hope this book will help you discover that happiness is accessible to you too!

Besides the culmination of life experience stories shared in this book, I also hold many certifications. I trained under Anthony Robbins and Cloe Madanes and got my certifications in Strategic Intervention and Marriage Education through the Robbins-Madanes Coach Training. (I learned a great deal about healthy relationships through this extensive training!) I also studied at Genesis Mind Coaching in Virginia and became a certified Nuero-Linguistic Programmer. Beyond the training, college credits, and certifications, I have always enjoyed learning "in the field" the best! I believe their is no substitute for experience!

CHAPTER 1

Love

"Love has no conditions, no boundaries, no limits, just an everlasting desire to put someone else's happiness first."
— Heather Paris

I define love as an action, or group of actions, that directly impacts and contributes to the well being of someone you care deeply for.

So many people cut themselves off from love because they have been hurt in the past. If you are one of them, I say, "STOP THAT! Love is amazing!" We all tend to put up walls. We start building them as young children any time we experience something painful. By the time we are adults, we have all sorts of walls and rigid conditions that go with them. When we set these conditions, we ultimately prevent ourselves from being vulnerable and experiencing all that life has to offer. We grow frightened and become reserved. We shelter ourselves, thinking we're being practical, when in fact we're disillusioning ourselves completely. Life doesn't really have to be that way!

We love our kids unconditionally but we rarely give that level of love to anyone else, including ourselves. We put conditions on our family and, especially, our spouses.

Love is about putting the needs of others before your own. Love is about allowing that person to be himself or herself without you trying to change them. Love is unselfish. It's about remaining constant and present even through the really difficult times. Love is about doing the little things, even when you're tired. It's about communicating honestly, even when you know it's going to hurt. Love is about holding each other, even when you don't feel like it. It's about hugging and kissing and holding hands and making love. Love is always putting one another first, before the kids, extended family or friends. Put your lover's needs before work, before phone calls, games and the Internet. Love is about being best friends. It's about listening and hearing and sharing it all. Love is about being free from judgment. Love is about laughing together, not at one another. Love is about being as close as two people can possibly be and letting nothing come between you. Love is about taking care of each other. But most of all, love is about doing all of these things all of the time. Don't stop until you take your last breath. Someone who is demonstrating true love would even walk away from their relationship if it meant the other person would be better off. Love isn't something you "fight to keep alive"; it is something you do to make someone else's life better.

Children often grow up and become involved in relationships similar to those they've seen modeled before them. Girls tend to marry men that treat them the way their own fathers treated their mothers and vice-versa. So teach love by living love. Put your relationship first; make it healthy and happy, give lots of affection, practice positive affirmations and kindness, and always put the needs of your partner ahead of your own. Your children will be happier knowing their parents have a solid foundation and will grow to emulate it.

Allowing oneself to become vulnerable to another person is not a weakness. We, as strong, independent people, often think that vulnerability equals weakness. But in actuality, vulnerability can be quite powerful. Men want to solve problems and fix things. They want to see their woman smile. It makes them feel needed and successful. So allow your man to "take care" of you. This idea is neither old-fashioned nor sexist. It is realistic. I'm not talking about women being "barefoot and pregnant" while a man takes care of your every need. I'm talking about telling a man exactly what you need - and allowing him to do things that will help you. For example: I COULD absolutely carry the heavy bags of horse feed into the barn from my car but I know that my husband would LOVE the opportunity to be helpful and do it for me. I used to have the attitude of "I will do it myself; I don't need help" but that is really not serving anyone. It actually disempowers ME because I am not allowing other people to give the gift of service and I am taking on an attitude of martyrdom.

A friend once told me that her boyfriend had disappointed her with his lack of action. Rather than tell him about her feelings and allow him the opportunity to make things right, she became defensive and quipped, "I will just do it myself. I have to do everything on my own. I have no one to count on."

I quickly reminded her that she was globalizing on a small incident and asked her what she was really feeling. When she said she was sad and wanted to cry, I told her she should have shared these feelings with him. She should have cried, and told her boyfriend why she was sad, and that he disappointed her. Her tears would have given him the visual queue that something was wrong. Then, she could have told him what was going on; giving him the opportunity to help her. They both would have felt better with this approach. A person is more likely to run from someone who is blaming or calling names and yelling. Conversely, they will be far more likely to jump up and help a loved one who is crying and clearly hurting.

Never trade love for comfort. You may be completely fearful of being "alone" but, do not stay in an abusive or unhealthy relationship because it is "better than being single." I cringe when I hear people say this. It saddens me to think that people feel they need to settle. When you get rid of the wrong people in your life, you make room for the right people!

As a rule of thumb, if you wouldn't accept an excuse from someone else, don't accept it for yourself. For example, if your daughter came home and told you she was in love with a married man and he claimed he HAD to stay with the wife because the timing was bad for him to leave her, what would you tell your daughter? You would let her know how absurd her words sound, for sure. Well, if it's not right, it's not right! Live with integrity and don't settle.

Again, I remind you, that in a successful relationship, you MUST put one another first. Not second to someone else's wife, kids, job, mistress, sports, video games, etc… FIRST. Love is something that you DO, and if you are "doing" someone or something else, you are not loving your partner! I will discuss "healthy break-ups" later in the book.

There are three types of love: Two that don't work and one that does.

1) Dependent Love. Dependent love says "What about ME? What have you done for me?" This type of love is not sustainable for very long. You can only take care of someone for so long before you become resentful and feel the need to have your own needs met.

2) Independent Love. Independent love says, "I don't NEED you! I can do it by myself!" This type of love is also not sustainable because the truth of the matter is, we all need other people. We all need to feel loved and have our needs met. This type of love is for martyrs who want to feel important, not loved.

3) Interdependent Love. Interdependent love says, "your needs are my needs and I strive to meet your needs always." This type of love is lasting. When you and your partner put one another first and always try to meet each others needs above your own, you are in a win-win relationship that always feels special and fulfilling.
(Types of love is from Robbins-Madanes Coach Training: http://www.rmtcenter.com/)

A life lesson in LOVE:

I was driving down the road on a cool, sunny morning when I noticed how beautiful the countryside was. I started to cry. There were tears in my eyes and a huge smile on my face. It was at this moment when I realized I was overwhelmed with a feeling in my heart. What was it? It was unfamiliar. At first, I thought it was merely an elevated sense of my usual feelings of contentment and happiness; when, in actuality, I was feeling love.

I moved to upstate New York so that my daughter, Madison, could attend a charter school. I chose a house in the country with four acres, a barn, and a pond. I wanted my children to experience the "country life" where we could enjoy horses and live in a peaceful environment.

After we moved into our dream home, I had a party, complete with a band and a houseful of teenagers, for Madison's 15th birthday. It was an awesome night and one that I will never forget. Why? Because that was the night I met Thad. Thad was the band "Dad" who transported all of the boy's instruments and equipment to my house. He poked his head into the doorway to set down an amplifier. As quickly as he peeked in, he slipped back out to grab the rest of the equipment. At that very moment, I KNEW we had a "cosmic connection." I had no idea how or why it developed, but I just knew we were going to be connected at a deeper level.

Thad and I became friends, spending the next two years flirting with each another. We developed an incredible friendship and every time we were together, we seemed to radiate an energy that was obvious to everyone else but us.

Our friendship developed to a point where I was comfortable enough to ask him for help with a homeless child I had taken under my wing. It was no longer possible for the boy to stay with me, so I asked Thad if he could stay with him. The boy was a friend to Thad's son. Thad agreed without hesitation. For the next several months we co-parented a child that didn't belong to either one of us. Thad was the kindest and most generous person I had ever met. He, much like me, gave freely without ever considering how it might impact his life. I knew he was truly selfless.

Shortly thereafter, Thad and I decided to get together with my roommate and her boyfriend to go out. After a fantastic evening, we stopped to admire the view from a hilltop field overlooking Ithaca, NY. We lay in the hay field looking up at the stars, my head resting on his shoulder and his arm around me. We still had no idea we were falling in love.

It was only a few days later that I was driving down

my country road with those tears in my eyes, smiling from ear to ear, full of love and life and inspiration. I was so full that when I got home, I started my "Live Inspired Now" blog. (www.liveinspirednow.com) I wanted to share my inspiration with the world. I wanted EVERYONE to live with the same passion and fullness that I was feeling. I wanted every single soul to feel the kind of love and excitement that was only just beginning to grow within me. I wanted them to realize that there are no second chances. You truly only live once. Letting it all pass you by is only a waste. To avoid risks, to not lay in a field, to not ride the shopping cart through the store parking lot, or ever admit that you are in love with someone is really not living at all. (Duh, I still had no idea I was in love! My heart knew but it didn't tell my head.) My very first post to the world was simply about lying in the grass, watching the clouds.

It took almost two weeks after that evening before I even realized I was in love! I stood in my bedroom crying, telling my roommates, "I LOVE THAD!" I could barely contain myself. I cried and laughed, saying over and over again, "I can't believe it! I'm in love with Thad!"

He was the reason why suddenly, everything looked brighter and life seemed more fun. My heart was swelling with emotion. He was the reason I couldn't pry the smile off of my face. He was the reason I felt so inspired each day! He was the motivation behind every blog post. Each post was about something I did with Thad or would love to do with Thad.

Shortly after my revelation, Thad called me and asked me out to lunch. I was thrilled when he asked me if I thought we had amazing chemistry and that we just clicked when we are together. I was beside myself and could barely contain my excitement. I had JUST figured out that I loved the man, and like a dream come true, he was sitting right before me telling me he "like-likes" me too! I wanted to leave to talk to him more because my overwhelming emotion was attracting the attention of the hostess. (Even today I notice people staring at us. I like to think it's because we really do resonate with one another on a cosmic level that emits an amazing energy that is pleasant to observe.)

So off to the car we went, talking for quite some time. We talked about the amazing connection we had and what great friends we were and that we were very much attracted to one another. And I was so nervous! Nonetheless, we agreed to go on our first "real" date that Saturday.

Thad and I spent the entire week texting, talking, "Facebooking", emailing, and communicating via any other means you can think of, leading up to our big date on Saturday. He picked me up and that was it. We have never been apart since. Our date was so sweet, too. We went to dinner then to the grocery store to race shopping carts. He challenged me to find the correct spelling of the word "roux" in one the cookbooks and stated that I would "win a kiss" if I had the correct spelling. Well, I found it and spelled it correctly which meant only one thing; our first kiss was only moments away! I was extremely nervous and thrilled at the same time!

We left the store and headed to "our spot," the same hill where we snuggled in the hay field a couple weeks prior. It was there that we shared our very first kiss. The kiss that I "won" fair and square! OMG, I was so nervous. I could feel my heart pounding just a little bit more than I could feel his heart jumping through his chest! It was magical. We kissed and hugged and talked and…talked more…and after several hours he finally brought me home. I was completely and hopelessly in love. That very night we decided to change our Facebook statuses to "in a relationship!" (Sign of the times! LOL)

When Thad got home that night, he sent me a Facebook message and told me "Heather Jane Deaville, I LOVE YOU!" I didn't want him to wait until morning to hear it back so I sent him a text message right away and told him I loved him too! Four months later we were engaged to be married. On the sixteenth of June 2011, I married my best friend!

We are so blessed to share a genuine love that is exciting and beautiful and full of passion and romance. We have dedicated our lives to making one another happy and raising our kids together. WOW. I love that man so much!! He truly in my inspiration!

QUICK TIPS:

~If you want love, give love. You will always feel what you give. The only way to attract love to your life is by giving and being love.

~We all make mistakes but choosing to love is never one of them.

~If you meet the needs of your partner and vice versa, you will have a love that will last.

CHAPTER 2

Healthy Break-Ups

"Life is beautiful and will continue to be,
if you choose to make it so!"
— Heather Paris

$\mathcal{I}$f your relationship consists of constant fighting and struggles, it is because you are not meeting one another's needs. I have seen people who stay because of the kids, religion, family, or just because they "love them too much to leave." These are just excuses. Not all relationships are meant to last and that's okay. What is not okay is staying in a miserable relationship because you are afraid of being alone. Or, you are afraid of losing your house or children. If you are staying in a relationship because of fear, nobody wins. It would be better to move forward and learn to be happy again rather than to stay in misery. Most importantly, if children are part of a failing relationship, please remember to put their needs first. Kids desperately need stability and security. They depend on their parents one-hundred percent to provide such security. When that security is rocked, their world can feel like it is turned upside down. It can be frightening when your entire existence changes, even if the prior existence was volatile. Speak honestly with your kids about what is going on with the family without blaming or name-calling. Kids should never be dragged through the mire of an unhealthy break up.

If you or your partner decides to part ways, do so with respect and not with resentment for what no longer is. Change is inevitable. You can either accept that and be happy or fight the reality of the situation and live a life of struggle. People get so global over break ups; they believe they will never ever find the right person or that they will never be happy again, for some time, I thought that too, but I was wrong. They often think they will never love or be able to trust again. Only when you can be happy without the relationship and you can love and trust, despite being hurt in the past, will you find a deep and truly meaningful love. Look at every relationship as a learning experience, maybe even as a lesson about what not to do again. You will most certainly learn something about yourself. For example, you stayed too long because you were afraid you might never find someone else. Whatever the reason, learn the lesson so you don't make the same mistakes in your next relationship! It is not fair to punish "Mr. Now" for "Mr. Past's" mistakes.

When the break up occurs, allow yourself time to heal. Keep your cool and don't act out. Relationships don't end badly; people just act badly when relationships end. Remember to keep your dignity. Don't stalk the person or talk badly about them (especially around any children). Don't try to get other people to dislike them, either. And never, ever broadcast your grievances on social media sites. Allow yourself time to mourn the relationship. Take time to reflect before moving on and respect that the person had a special place in your heart at one time. The relationship may be over but your self-respect and the emotional well being of any children involved should remain intact, even if the other person is acting badly. You do not have to participate in other people's drama. Do not engage if your ex-partner is behaving badly. People leave our lives, whether voluntarily or involuntarily, so that we can make room for the right people.

Also, remember to listen to your intuition and make better choices. We are all guilty of allowing people into our lives that don't really deserve to be there. Instead, we should raise our standards and make better choices. If, while you are dating someone, you have to continually convince yourself that he or she is "going to change" or that you can "fix" them, you should terminate the relationship immediately! You are not in a good or healthy relationship and you are not being a good partner, either. Relationships are about meeting one another's needs. It's about putting one another first, not about trying to fix or change someone. The more people you try to fix, the more break-ups you will have and the more cynical you will become as you begin erecting walls to keep people out; this is no way to enter into a healthy relationship. So, do yourself a favor. Have healthy break ups, let go of the past, and move forward so that you can find that perfect partner that will be your true love.

A life lesson in HEALTHY BREAK UPS:

When my very first boyfriend, "Louie," and I broke up at age 17, I was devastated. I knew it was for the best; he was involved in drugs and I was a member of Students Against Driving Drunk (SADD). Nonetheless, I really felt like I loved him. We went our separate ways in high school, but years later we were re-acquainted by way of a mutual friend. We decided go to a friend's wedding together and spend some time getting caught up. Well, we talked and laughed for hours! We decided that although the break-up seemed devastating at the time to our young passionate 17-year-old selves, in hindsight, it wasn't really all that bad. We simply parted ways, never speaking badly about one another, never regretting the relationship, and understanding that we were just going in different directions at the time. I suppose it was easier to split up back in 1989 because there was no Internet, no Facebook, no cell phones and no quick access to stalk one another. So I suppose in all fairness, break ups were easier twenty-some years ago. But, the standards remain true today.

Louie and I remained friends for years after that but eventually lost touch. I hope he is living a happy and healthy life. Not every break up in my life has gone as smoothly, but I've always believed in leaving a relationship like a boy scout leaves a campsite: "Leave it better than you found it!"

QUICK TIPS:
~Time will heal the hurt feelings. Allow yourself time to mourn the relationship.
~Make peace with what has happened in your past before moving on.
~Always maintain dignity and treat others the way you want to be treated.

CHAPTER 3

Good vs. Bad Designations

"When we stop assigning good or bad value to
events, feelings, and people we become free from
needless suffering caused by our own beliefs!"
— Heather Paris

People love to assign a value of good or bad to everything. But, what if things aren't good or bad — what if they just are?

There is a Taoist story that I love about an old farmer who worked his crops for many years. One day his horse ran away. Upon hearing the news, his neighbors came to visit.

"Such bad luck," they said sympathetically.

"Maybe," the farmer replied.

The next morning the horse returned, bringing with it three other wild horses.

"How wonderful," the neighbors exclaimed.

"Maybe," replied the old man.

The following day, his son tried to ride one of the untamed horses but he was thrown and broke his leg. The neighbors again came to offer their sympathy on his misfortune.

"Maybe," answered the farmer.

The day after, military officials came to the village to draft young men into the army. Seeing that the son's leg was broken, they passed him by. The neighbors congratulated the farmer on how well things had turned out.

"Maybe," said the farmer.

This story is a perfect example of how we create value for things without ever thinking about how they might make us feel differently. We draw conclusions about situations without seeing the bigger picture. Good things can come from tragedy and bad things can happen during the best of times. People step up during tragedies and emerge as leaders and heroes. Sometimes tragedy provides us with an opportunity for change that might not have otherwise been there. For example, I have a friend who viewed her cancer as a blessing because it taught her to value her life more. She saw the illness as an opportunity to make lifestyle changes; without these changes she would have most certainly died. She felt blessed with a new, positive outlook that didn't exist prior to the diagnosis.

Another example is when two people are diagnosed with the same disease, like breast cancer. One woman may look at it negatively, become depressed and eventually die from the illness. Another may use the illness to become a champion for the cause, raise money for research and ultimately become a role model for other cancer patients and survivors.

We have all heard stories of people that survive horrible circumstances as children and still emerge as great leaders who accomplish amazing things. On the other end of the spectrum, there are cases of extremely privileged people who have everything handed to them and they grow up unhappy with no real purpose, often addicted to drugs, alcohol or other unhealthy choices.

The choices we make are always our own. We get to decide how we view things. Will they be good or bad? Will they empower us or hold us back? Will our circumstances be part of our success story or our excuse? You are not your circumstances; you can rise above anything. All you have to do is give your story a different meaning.

Not long ago, I hired a teenager to help me clean out my rental property. He was a friend to our family and he was very happy for the opportunity to earn some cash. He had recently dropped out of high school and I really wanted to help him get back on track. He had experienced many hardships growing up, from poverty to abuse, but nonetheless was a great kid with a great personality. He had a positive attitude and an unbelievable dedication to health and fitness. I wanted him to see that the hardship he was facing would only continue if he didn't at least pursue his high school diploma. Despite the fact he had been classified as ADHD/ADD with emotional issues, and received special accommodations for his "disability", I wanted this young man to see he was more than just a label – he was an intelligent human being that could accomplish anything.

One of the things I wanted this young man to do for me was to wash the kitchen floor. I asked him whether he wanted to use a mop or a toothbrush. "Why would I use a toothbrush?" he asked me. "It would be too hard. A mop would be easier." "Why would you start your adult life without a high school diploma when it would be so much easier to go through life with one?" I retorted.

I explained that while he could definitely "get by" washing the kitchen floor with a toothbrush, he could also "get by" without the diploma. But wouldn't it be so much easier with the right tool? He got it, but he claimed he lacked one thing that could get him back to school: motivation.

"Look at your body," I said to him. "You have fifteen percent body fat. Your muscles are toned and sculpted and you are very strong. How did you get that way?"

He went on to vaguely explain that he works out. I explained that if he has the motivation and determination to work out daily, he could also find the motivation to go back to school. Every single day he finds a way to the gym. He rips his muscles continually to allow them to build up and become bigger and stronger. He dedicates himself to a clean and healthy lifestyle, never wavering from his high standards. He lifts more and more weight each week to become stronger. On days when he doesn't feel like exercising, he works harder, never lowering his standards for his body and health. As a result of his dedication and determination, he has a body to be proud of and a clean lifestyle. Many kids his age lack motivation and choose to fill their time with unhealthy activities, yet he possesses motivation that few adults have, let alone teenagers.

Once he realized what I was saying, he was shocked. He never realized the self-determination he actually had. He stood before me, a bit taller, with his newfound understanding and sense of accomplishment. I told him he was a true leader and should be proud of his accomplishments. I told him I was proud of him, but he should be proud of himself. We talked about his goals, what he wanted to do with those goals, and how he could accomplish them.

After our talk, he has a renewed sense of what he should be doing with his life. He asked me to help him get back into school and I did. He went back to high school, and was bringing in A's and B's. The school has also removed his special education classification. The teachers told me they could not believe he was the same kid. His resource teacher suggested he take several honors classes. Today, he is a high school graduate and is now looking into colleges and working to become a physical trainer.

I do not believe this young man was ever ADD/ADHD. I believe he is a kinesthetic learner; a student that learns by doing, exploring, and discovering. Unfortunately, the traditional educational system does not support this learning style. However, his resource teacher allowed him to stand up and move while working and even allowed him to do handstands and cartwheels, as needed.

This young man doesn't see his life circumstances as good or bad. He just sees them as learning opportunities and lessons to take into the future. Nobody would ever want another person to suffer, but I truly believe that hardships shape us. What will you take from the lessons life provides? Life becomes so much less painful when you let go of good and bad and embrace that life just happens. Right and wrong are subjective and life isn't fair, but it is still good. Looking back, some of the things that happened in my life that I thought were so horrible at the time turned out to be blessings in disguise. Accept that there is a bigger picture and that we don't always get to know the whole story. Allow the Universe to provide for you and believe that things always work out the way they should.

A life lesson in GOOD AND BAD DESIGNATIONS:

I grew up as an "Army Brat". My dad was in the Army for twenty-five years, which afforded us the opportunity to live in some really great places. My favorite place was Germany. We lived there on and off until I was almost eleven, moving back to the U.S. in the early 80s.

While we lived in Hanau, Germany, I was in elementary school. The school was located in a separate military housing complex, requiring me to walk to and from school each day. Looking back, it seemed like a very long walk, at least four miles, but in reality, it was probably about a half mile or less. Each day my best friend, Joanne, and I would walk to school, climbing through a wooded area that we named "Monkey Hills." We shared stories about boys and all the fun things we were going to do after school.

We used to walk on these really funny walls that were built with green sacs all around the military housing. The walls came up to my chest. We would try to do cartwheels along them on our way to school. What I didn't know was that the walls were actually sandbags and protected us civilians from possibly getting shot by terrorists. I look back now and think about how crazy it was that I had no idea they were put there to protect us. My friends and I just thought they were cool walls for us to play on; again, it's all about the meaning we give to things. My parents could have told us what was going on but they didn't want to scare us. They simply kept a close eye on us so we could enjoy our youthful innocence, as much as possible, in a volatile world.

We got a new school too! I was super excited because they built it in our own housing area so I wouldn't have to walk "all that way" anymore. What I didn't realize was that we were getting a new school because there was a bombing very close to the old school that left it damaged. I think it was the Non-Commissioned Officer's Club that had been bombed but I don't remember because I had an entirely different picture of what was going on.

My Mom brought me over to the new school site as it was being built. She got me excited about the new building and how close it was. We watched the progress daily and never once did any of the adults let us really know why the new school was being built.

This memory reminds me of my favorite movie "Life Is Beautiful", starring Roberto Benigni. In the movie, a family is imprisoned and taken to a concentration camp. Throughout the entire movie, Roberto Benigni hides his young son, convincing the boy that the entire ordeal is a game. He further tells him that in order to get the most points and win the game, he must stay hidden from the German soldiers and follow his fathers rules at all times. In the end, the young son and his mother both survive and the young boy never realizes the experience for the true hardship it was. It was a breathtaking movie and I highly recommend it.

Another great example is in Viktor Frankl's book "Man's Search for Meaning." In the book, Frankl chronicles his time in a concentration camp; he talks about blessings, lessons learned, faith, and survival. Frankl was able to overcome his circumstances and use the experiences to write a book that inspires millions with his story.

While my personal experience in Germany was nothing compared to being in a concentration camp, the idea is still the same: we choose how to feel about our circumstances, good or bad.

Frankl said, "Everything can be taken from a man or a woman but one thing: the last of human freedoms to choose one's attitude in any given set of circumstances, to choose one's own way."

QUICK TIPS:

~Things aren't good or bad, they just are.

~Life isn't fair, it's not supposed to be, but it is good!

~If you can't change a situation, change how you feel or think about it!

CHAPTER 4

Discharge

"Discharge negative feelings, emotions, or experiences
daily, so as not to carry them forward as baggage!
— Heather Paris

D ischarge is the release of emotional baggage
that allows you to move forward. Sometimes
you just have to discharge those negative feelings that
you have. We all get them; and part of living a happy
life is to get them out of our system and not live with
them. Discharging negative feelings is very freeing and
will make you feel so much better. You will feel like a
load has been lifted off your shoulders! Even optimistic
people like me have feelings of anger, disappointment,
and sadness, but the key is to let those feelings out when
you feel them and move forward with joy, happiness,
and love. Holding on to negativity is unhealthy and
can manifest into physical problems, like high blood

pressure, anxiety, and even cancer. So, let yourself go. Tell your significant other or best friend to just listen and let it all out. Scream and shout, cry and complain, or even break something if you have to. Just let it all GO.

Sometimes breaking things is a good thing! Do you have old computer parts (hard drive or CD's) that need to be destroyed? Is there a pile of wood outside that needs to be chopped? Or, even some leftover boxes from Christmas that need to be broken down? It can be very therapeutic to break things or destroy things as long as it is done in a safe and non-harmful way. It is great exercise both mentally and physically, as well. Personally, I learned to break boards with my hands and that is so EMPOWERING! My kids did it too! We took pine boards and wrote our fears or frustrations on them and broke the boards in half. I recommend learning how to do this safely first before trying it.

My husband and I spend time telling one another about our day and that often involves some discharging. We talk about any challenges that we faced. We often have nothing at all to discharge about; that means it was a great day!

Get to learn your partner's queues too. Every now and then something will upset me. If I don't feel like talking about it, my husband always knows. Sometimes he will ask, "Would you like to discharge or do you need time alone?" In rare cases, I will be so upset that my husband will actually push me to discharge and talk to him, even though I don't want to. He is always spot on when this happens. Everyone discharges in a different way, but the key is to get it out and not hold on to anger, sadness, or hurt feelings.

There have been a couple of times when my husband was very upset about something, but he was unable to get the words out. He said he wanted to discharge but didn't really know what to say. I asked him if he wanted me to discharge for him and he said yes. So I yelled and screamed about the situation and reflected how upset "I" was, and how angry "I" felt. After that, he felt great! He smiled and said, "That is exactly right and now "I" feel better!" We laughed after that.

Laughing is also another great way to discharge. Sometimes when we are faced with situations we have no control over, laughing about it can be a huge relief. Thad and I try to laugh as much as possible. Laughing is good exercise as well as good for your physical and mental health. Being silly is great for you too. The more fun you have, the fewer things will bother you. That means less time spent discharging!

I have created an acronym for FUN - Frequently Unleashing Nonsense. So have FUN wherever you are! Thad and I are often completely ridiculous when we go out. During one grocery shopping adventure, we made the visit a blast by playing shopping cart basketball. One person throws the items; the other catches them in the cart. We often have other shoppers cheering for us; one man threw his arms in the air every time we would "sink a shot into the basket." We also ride the shopping cart and chat with other shoppers. We actually had a store employee cracking up because our laughter was contagious. In the end, the cashier said playfully that he was jealous of our love.

You owe it to yourself to live an inspired life full of happiness and joy. When you do experience pain, be sure to discharge it promptly so you can get back to having as much fun as possible!

A life lesson in DISCHARGE:

I started my blog a couple of years ago to give readers a daily dose of inspiration; but also used it as a way for me to discharge all the energy and love that I was feeling. I was in love with Thad and I was overflowing with joy and love and I needed a place to get that all out. It is a place where people can go for some real world examples of inspired life and daily reminders to live life to the fullest. (www.liveinspirednow.com)

I've always wanted to write a book but I repeatedly created excuses as to why it would never happen. None of the excuses were relevant; they were just excuses, which I fully admit. I used the blog as a means to write without the daunting task of actually penning an entire book. It was also instantly rewarding. I put my daily posts on Facebook and Twitter and received feedback from people who really liked what I had to say. It was a great way to get my thoughts and feelings out. At the time I started my blog, I was a single Mom, not yet fully aware that Thad was the love of my life, so we didn't talk on a daily basis. It was a great place for me to "talk" during what seemed like a kind of lonely time. I have friends and family but I've always been a private person and not one to "complain" outwardly about things. So I would often share only the good parts of my life, never leaning on anyone or opening up about my challenges or fears. The blog was a great means of expression for me. It seemed like I was telling my personal stories without really getting too personal and it made me feel great.

As time went on, I took more and more liberties with my writing; sharing even more and daring to put my opinion out there, even if I thought it might be unpopular. It was more than just discharging for me; it was a validation of my own feelings, too. My whole life I have told others that they were perfectly valid to express their thoughts and feelings, but I never really expressed or validated my own. The blog helped me to do just that. It opened me up, but more than that, it helped me gain more confidence and taught me that I am as valuable as I make everyone else feel. You can find my daily inspirations at www.liveinspirednow.com. I hope you are able to find some inspiration! Today, my blog posts are published in The Citizen newspaper (http://auburnpub.com/blogs/live_inspired_now/) and I submit my posts to different online and in print magazines as well.

QUICK TIPS:
~Talk about your day with someone you care about... everyday!
~Do not store scary or bad thoughts, feelings, or emotions. You have to release them to be free of them.
~Journaling, blogging, or personal diaries are awesome ways to discharge your feelings.
~Discharge stress and tension by having F.U.N. (Frequently unleashing nonsense!)
~Life is short, let go of that which doesn't enhance you and enjoy!

CHAPTER 5

Honesty

"Be honest or be lonely. Nobody likes a liar."
— Heather Paris

*H*onesty is being truthful, sincere, and refusing to manipulate situations for personal gratification. This is one of my least favorite topics but it needs to be talked about. I have such a hang up about lying; yet admittedly, I am not perfect and have lied before in my past. We all have. However, when we realize how much easier life becomes when we are completely honest, we can begin to make better choices.

Always be truthful. It is far more important to be honest and deal with fallout than it is to lie and manipulate. Lies always have a way of coming out and they will adversely affect you or those you love. You can find temporary comfort in lies, but true love, real emotions, integrity and honor come from honesty. You may get what you want from lying, but it will never last. The truth is permanent and freeing.

Often people lie or manipulate to get someone to "like" or "love" them. When we work to deceive people, we are really working against ourselves. When we lie or manipulate others, it degrades who we are. Lying perpetuates a degradation of personal morals. True love is generous and giving and not about what or who we can get. It is about what we can give and how we can help others. When you lie about who you are or don't fully share the truth about yourself, you are really telling yourself that you are not good enough just the way you are. You are also telling the other person that you don't trust them enough to like the real you.

When we love another person, we should love them whether they love us back or not; this is real love. It is not always reciprocated, but love built on lies, manipulation or guilt will never, ever last.

A young person I was working with once was so desperate to "keep his love" that he would tell the girl he was with just about anything so she would not leave him. He professed his undying love, asking her to marry him. He told her he wouldn't take a job she didn't approve of. He told her she could make all the decisions for their relationship. Then, he went behind her back and did whatever he wanted anyway. I told him he was not giving her the thing she really wanted, which was his authentic self. He was not making choices that were backed by integrity. She did eventually see through his facade and broke up with him. This young man learned a valuable lesson. He now makes honesty, even when it's hard, the cornerstone of his interactions. He learned the hard way that building a relationship upon a foundation of lies will end a relationship with pain.

Personality is often mistaken for integrity. People may think that just because someone is funny or pleasant, they have integrity. Just because a person is friendly or charming or has charisma, does not mean they are living with integrity. It is important to value integrity over personality. I know someone who is typically grumpy and not very easy to talk to, but nonetheless, that person is extremely reliable and would give the shirt off of his back for anyone at any time.

People with integrity are always honest and trust worthy. A person whose best quality is their personality may talk badly about you behind your back and look out for their own best interests, no matter how fun they appear to be. At the same time, don't discount people with integrity just because their personality may need "a little work". Likewise, don't keep people around who are unhealthy and dishonest just because they are charming.

I encourage everyone to speak honestly to their

children. This can be difficult when we don't want to share things we think will be painful for them; we want to protect them. However, the truth is always best. I've made many mistakes in my life and I discuss them openly with my kids so they may learn from them. Hopefully, they will not repeat these same mistakes. There are no guarantees, but I want to offer the best chances for success that I can.

My oldest daughter Madison's father is a recovering alcoholic and drug abuser. Madison knows this. I thought that it was better for her to know the truth than to make up reasons as to why she thought her dad acted certain ways. When she was younger and he and I were still married, he went into rehab several times. Each time we visited him, I told Madison, "Daddy has some challenges to overcome and if he will work hard toward getting better, we will support him". You can use age appropriate words but the truth is the best policy, even when they are young.

As she grew older, she understood that her dad was an alcoholic and had used drugs. When he was clean, we were supportive and encouraging. When he was not, he had to make his own choices and they were his alone to make. Madison and her dad are very close and she is compassionate towards him. I believe she has learned from his bad choices. She is also encouraging and supportive to other teenagers who are struggling with addictions. I wouldn't be surprised if one day she became a counselor of some sort.

Hiding scary life situations from children can be extremely detrimental to them. When they grow older, they may live the same kinds of problems, and if nobody validates what they are going through, it may make them feel isolated. A child can see, hear, and feel all of the drama in the house, whether it be fighting, addiction issues, affairs, depression, isolation, or even just tension. Kids experience it too! I often hear people say "we don't fight in front of the kids," or "the kids didn't know that mom was using drugs," or "the kids didn't know dad was sleeping around." To this I must say bullshit! Kids DO know what's going on. They might not know the details but they feel the tension and hear the fighting. They can see that their parents don't touch or kiss each other or even smile. Kids are extremely perceptive. Trying to cover it up only makes them feel like they are crazy or their feelings aren't valid or that they aren't important enough to be talked to. Kids can handle it! Talk to them! There is absolutely nothing wrong with being honest with children. If their father has an issue with drinking, be honest. Say, "Dad has a problem with alcohol. It is a grown up drink that makes you stumble and impairs judgment. Dad wants to get help and we will support his efforts. I'm sorry you had to see him falling down, but that is what alcohol does. We hope he is able to overcome this, but it is up to him."

Or, "Dad lost his job and with Mom not working, we are struggling and are a little nervous about things right now. You can help though. You can remember to turn off lights, and maybe help Mom clip coupons. I don't want you to worry. Mom and Dad will get through this. Sometimes we might get a little cranky; that is not your fault but we appreciate your help!"

Another example: "I'm sorry you heard us fighting last night. We were yelling and that must have been very scary. We shouldn't have done that. Sometimes parents get mad and sometimes they argue, but it's just because we disagree about something. We will try and work it out in a less scary manner. We just want you to know your feelings are valid and we apologize for scaring you."

These statements are fact, not opinion. So, if you or your spouse is having difficulties, you can let your kids know what is going on. However, calling the other person names or insulting them, in the presence of your kids, is not acceptable. Children can handle information but should never have to deal with being turned against another parent.

You can explain situations to your kids without giving all the details. When you do this, it leaves them with a sense of knowing rather than compounding the chaos of living in the dark. I also think it is imperative to apologize to your kids. Of course, we are not perfect and we do make mistakes. However, it is invaluable for the kids to see you apologize, when necessary. It sets a wonderful example.

Don't force kids to apologize. A forced apology is no better than a lie. I hear parents say all the time, "Tell him you're sorry now!" That forced apology only shows the child that words are magic erasers. But they are not. Instead, explain the wrong that occurred. Explain how the other person might feel and then ask the child what they want to do about it. Let your kids know that although they are not responsible for how other people feel they are responsible for their own words and actions. Sometimes the things we say impact other people. The words "I'm sorry" following an offense are hollow if there are no feelings of remorse to back them up.

At some point in their lives, kids will learn to lie. This is an age appropriate behavior for young children. To combat this, consistently remind them that honesty is not only the best policy, but is the only policy that will yield true happiness.

A life lesson in HONESTY:

Oh, I really hate to share this story because my parents never did learn the truth, but here goes nothing!

When I was 8 or 9, I got in trouble for calling another little girl a bad word. I denied it so well that my parents believed me! Here's the story:

We lived in Germany at the time. I was walking home from school one day and there was this little girl who was being really rotten to a bunch of kids. She was picking on them and being mean and bossy. As self appointed, "champion to the down trodden," I felt I had no choice but to intervene. In the flurry of name-calling and back and forth insult spewing, I blurted out a phrase that I had heard the older kids in my neighborhood use: "You are a DILDO!"

Everyone kind of ganged up on her and the barrage of insults was enough to make her stop harassing the others. It was MY insult she remembered though, and she ran home and told her parents. Now I had heard this word from a group of older boys that used to hang out on the stoop in my neighborhood. They never said it to me and I have no idea in what context they were even using the word, but I heard it enough to know it was bad. I didn't intend to internalize the word, but apparently, I put that little gem in my arsenal and just waited until I could use it, then when the opportunity was there... BLAM!

Later that evening there was a knock at the door. I opened it to find the little girl with her parents. I stood frozen in horror, certain I was about to die. My parents came up behind me and said, "May I help you?"

Do you remember the Charlie Brown cartoons and how the teacher never actually spoke words? You just heard that funny sound, "wont wont wont wont wont?" That is similar to what I heard, except it was more like: "wont wont wont DILDO wont wont wont!"

My parents looked down at me and asked, "Did you say that word?"

"No," I responded promptly.

My parents politely defended me and that was it. They excused the accusers from our doorstep and shut the door. Oh my goodness, my parents were so furious that I would be accused of such a heinous crime! The story doesn't end there...

A few weeks later I was sitting at the dining room table with the dictionary. I wanted to know what "dildo" meant.

In walked my mother and asked, "Heather, what are you looking up?" In an attempt to cover my tracks, I stumbled, "Nothing...err...something for school. Um... err...I don't really know. It's nothing really."

She knew something was askew and kept prodding me to find out what it was. Finally, with tears in my eyes, I said, "I don't know what dildo means."

My mother took the dictionary away and asked why

I was looking it up. I told her I heard it for the first time when the other parents had come over and I didn't know what it meant. SHE BELIEVED ME! I truly couldn't believe it. I thought I was about to die for looking up that word, but she believed me. Then, she did her best to explain such a taboo word to a young person. After learning what it was, I was too grossed out to utter it again. I always felt badly that I had lied about that, though.

So my dear parents, now you know and I apologize for lying to you! I respect the integrity you live with and thank you for raising me to know that lying is not the way. I am grateful for this lesson because although I did lie from time to time, I knew it was wrong and was able to feel bad about it. This shaped who I am today.

QUICK TIPS:

~Lies hurt people. They are hard to keep up with and they push people away.

~Respect children enough to be honest with them. Tell them the truth about situations without making judgments or rude comments about those involved.

~Don't lie to your parents; even if you get away with it, you will feel badly.

CHAPTER 6

Sex

"Sex is an important part of any healthy, happy, committed
relationship and should be shared freely and daily!"
— Heather Paris

S ex is the physical intimacy shared between two
beings. Every person on earth needs physical
touch, love and companionship. Sharing an intimate
relationship with someone is a beautiful expression of
love and trust. It connects us emotionally to our lover
and creates a strong attachment. A healthy sex life also
creates passion and playfulness and can strengthen a
relationship. Don't let a day go by where you are not
intimate with your partner in some way. It doesn't have
to be sex. It can be a hug, holding each other, snuggles,
kisses, touching, or just playfulness. Lack of intimacy
can make a person feel lonely or isolated. Physical touch

actually produces oxytocin, dopamine, and serotonin which create feelings of joy and elation!

A healthy, passionate relationship can also be a good example for our children. It is good for them to see parents smile when they see one another and to see a relationship where there is lots of hugging and kissing and passion.

I believe in talking openly and honestly with kids about sex and intimacy. They need to know what is real about sex; not what they hear on the school bus. I am always astounded when I hear older teens telling me what they think they know about sexual relations. I've heard things like, "You can't get pregnant if you go to the bathroom afterwards," or "If I don't have sex then I won't get a boyfriend," or, "All boys like to have sex, that's just how it is."

OMG.... REALLY? Who is talking to these kids? Please start talking to your children about this when they are young and continue to expand upon the subjects as they mature. Be sure to tell them what your moral values are on the subject. For example, I tell my children that masturbation is natural and normal. Nobody talks openly about it and I feel it's important. I personally don't think children under the age of eighteen should be having sex, as I don't feel that they are emotionally or physically ready to handle it. Some kids are so desperate to feel love and connection, they have sex. When the relationship ends, they feel hopeless. Often they understand they have lost an experience they should have waited to share. I tell my kids they must be in a long-term, healthy committed relationship with one partner and be out of high school. Until then, I encourage them to "take care of their own needs" because I realize that they still have raging hormones and lots of sexual desires. When they are able to take care of their own needs they never have to worry about disease or pregnancy or the emotional pain associated with growing up too fast. Also, when speaking with kids about sex, use the proper words. Studies show that kids who are confident and knowledgeable about sex and their own bodies are less likely to be molested or abused because they know what is appropriate and what is not. Protect kids by giving them knowledge about sex. Help them make healthy choices. Don't act like it's an embarrassing subject to talk about. You want them to feel comfortable coming to you. Set moral guidelines for what you feel is acceptable for your children and your family.

For yourself, if you don't have a healthy attitude about sex and intimacy, seek a counselor or life coach and get past the issue. Many women in particular, who have faced some sort of sexual abuse in their life hold on to that experience and allow it to prevent them from opening up fully and enjoying a healthy sex life. Many men also don't fully understand how to "woo" a woman and how to make her feel safe enough to give her entire body. Work to get past whatever holds you back from enjoying a healthy sexual relationship. Do it for your relationship and do quickly.

Don't hold on to pain and lock it deep away to "keep it safe." What do you lock up in a safe? Things of value or importance like jewelry, money, or important documents. When you put painful memories in a "safe place" in your soul, you are subconsciously doing the same thing. This gives the painful event or memory power and is guaranteed to continue to cause further suffering. If you are trying to get past something traumatic, like rape or molestation, the worst thing you could do is lock it away so you don't have to "deal with it." If you want to overcome something painful, talk about it, write about it, and share your story to get it out. Take away the power of the memory by not holding on to it. Allow yourself to be free from the pain associated with the event or memory to the point where it becomes mere history. Now you can tell the story without shame, fear, pain, grief, or whatever else you may have assigned to it. You will not only feel free, but you will experience joy, closeness and intimacy again.

You deserve a happy and healthy sex life and all the happiness of a passionate relationship!

A life lesson in SEX:

Again, I encourage you to speak to your children about sex and healthy sexual relationships, as well as their bodies and how they work. Do you remember the first talk YOU got? I don't because I don't remember getting a talk. The only thing I remember is a conversation when I was in 7th grade. I was just about to go upstairs to bed when my father called out to me. He and my mother were on the couch as I stood looking at them from the staircase.

"One of these days you're going to bleed, um, you know, down there," my father stammered nervously. "If it happens at school, wad up some toilet paper and stuff it in there and tell your Mom when you get home."

That was it.

I went to bed completely horrified that my "down there" was going to bleed. Even worse, I would have to come home and tell my Mom after it happens? WHAT THE HELL? We never really talked about these things and so I didn't really know what the hell he was talking about anyway. Lucky for me, my Mom had been purchasing pads and hiding them in the linen closet so when I did get my period for the first time, I could just take one from the secret stash that seemed to replenish magically. Thank goodness!

When I became a parent, I vowed to talk to my kids about sex and masturbation and periods and everything else that goes along with puberty. I promised myself to be matter-of-fact and handle it all like it was no big deal. And that is just what I did. Because of this, every one of my kids knows how it all works and even use the proper terminology when discussing these topics. They know that masturbation is natural and normal and the preferred method of sexual expression until they become adults and are mature enough to commit to long-term relationships. They know what will happen to their bodies and that it is part of growing up and becoming a healthy adult. I am grateful for my parent's discomfort in talking about these things because it created the attitude of openness I now have with my own children.

QUICK TIPS:

~Sex and intimacy are part of a healthy, happy, and passionate relationship. ~Overcome sexual dysfunction and free yourself.

~Speak openly and honestly about sex with your children so they will be less likely to be the victim of a sexual predator and grow with a healthy attitude about sex.

CHAPTER 7:

Education

"Stop educating children to perpetuate mediocrity. Inspire them to greatness by igniting them with joy, dazzling them with beautiful art, amusing them with wit, and encouraging their creativity to flow freely. Raise masterpieces."
— Heather Paris

*E*ducation is the art of acquiring useful knowledge that will benefit you for the rest of your life. I am rather opinionated on the subject of our modern educational system and how it seems as if we try to discourage children from learning. The current system tends to merely focus on being able to pass state exams rather than teaching children how to live exceptional lives. It kills me to see kids who are really smart and creative feel like complete failures because people aren't recognizing the way they are smart. Figuring out your child's learning style can be a huge step in helping them succeed.

Learning styles are the ways in which we learn and receive information. The most common model is "Neil Fleming's VAK model." VAK stands for visual, auditory, and kinesthetic. (For more detailed information, please visit www.vark-learn.com.) The VAK model is the most basic and easy to understand but there are more comprehensive models that break the learning styles down even further. The VAK model is as follows: Visual learners will learn better by looking at pictures, videos, graphs, diagrams or other visual tools. They like to see things and learn with their eyes. Auditory learners will learn better by listening to things such as audio books, cd's, lectures or speakers. They like to hear things and learn with their ears. Kinesthetic learners will learn better by using a hands-on approach, touching things, using movement and participating in activities like experiments or labs. They like to feel things and learn with their actions. Finding out your child's learning style will give you and their teachers a better insight on how to help them learn. A kinesthetic learner (like me) may feel overwhelmed when a lesson is verbally explained to them yet if you show them how to do something they will pick right up on it.

My kinesthetic daughter Carrie started to do better in her math class last year when her teacher let her stand up to do her assignments. It is all about figuring out how they learn, working with it and then finding ways for them to feel successful. There is more than one way to measure success and I think it is imperative that we offer kids multiple ways to be successful.

I never received good grades as a child. It wasn't that I wasn't smart enough; it was just that I learned differently. Quite frankly, I was bored at school. I could never understand why on earth anyone would want to sit still for six straight hours and learn things that I felt had little practical value? My parents tried everything with me. I was grounded for a year once because of a bad report card. They punished me by taking away my privileges. Then they tried bribing me, paying me, embarrassing me, and even lecturing me. The fact was, I hated school. No matter what they did or said, I didn't improve. This was the theme of my entire school career and it never changed. I started college thinking it would be different. I figured I would be in control and could come and go as I pleased. But it wasn't control I was seeking. I was actually looking for a place that was suitable to a kinesthetic learner and valued thinkers instead of what I call "regurgitators."

One of my favorite quotes is from Albert Einstein: "Everyone is a genius, but if you judge a fish on its ability to climb a tree, it will live its whole life believing it is stupid." In my later years I realized I loved to learn and became more than capable of exceeding course expectations and doing well as a student. I just needed someone to take the time to recognize that I learned differently and that I was a creative thinker.

I believe that schools today teach antiquated facts, expecting kids to memorize them and spit them back. I feel this is less than useful in today's world. We need kids to learn how to be creative, think openly, and problem solve. Why on earth would anyone need to memorize useless facts when you have a wealth of information at your instant disposal at all times? In my opinion, the biggest focus at school should be reading ability. If they can read, the world is open to them and they can learn anything! Children today need to learn how to read and understand language well. They need to fully understand the importance of health and wellness. They need to understand computers and be able to use the Internet proficiently, all while mastering the ever-changing world of smart phones and other technologies. Most importantly, they need to learn social intelligence. In our modern world a fact memorizer is useless. We have search engines for that. What is indispensable are people who can present themselves well, are well spoken, have the ability to adapt to every situations, and make quick and effective decisions while honing skills of compassion, kindness, and altruism. I believe the best education comes from experience and when we limit kids to a classroom environment only we rob them of valuable hands on experiences and culture. There needs to be a change!

I also believe we need to teach our kids better values. They don't teach this in schools, so it is imperative we teach them at home. Kindness and respect are not subjects at school. Having them learn "life skills" from children on the school bus is not the way to educate them. It is my thought that all kids should be "home schooled," even if they go to regular school. It is up to us to impart our values, manners and social skills to our children. It is up to us to teach them about grooming and hygiene. We need to teach them proper table settings, how to order and eat at a buffet versus a five-star restaurant, how to be generous and giving, how to put others first without compromising themselves, how to make a polite phone call and interact appropriately, how to compliment someone the right way, and how to self advocate. We especially need to teach our kids how to speak for themselves and treat themselves with respect, as well as others.

I work with so many teenagers that think they are useless, have no self worth or confidence and end up making very risky choices because they don't believe they deserve better. Don't assume because you don't say negative things that a child will in turn believe in only positive things about themselves. You have to tell them they are smart and beautiful and allow them opportunities to shine, as well as the opportunity to fail!

Teach them to learn. Sheltering children from pain doesn't protect them from the world. In fact, it makes them more vulnerable. Instead, teach children how to deal with pain and disappointment in a healthy way. Teach them to communicate their true feelings, teach them to allow themselves time to feel badly and then to move forward without carrying the baggage of past hurts with them. This will teach children how to overcome challenges without giving up. It will equip them with the skills they need to persevere in life. Toddlers fall down many times before they learn to walk. You wouldn't hold a child back from learning to walk just because they might fall. In the same way, continue to allow your child to "fall" as they get older. These are life lessons that will shape their destiny and make them stronger and more capable. Don't protect your child from natural consequences. Allow them to learn valuable lessons that only come from experience. While they are learning, always let them know you are there if they need you.

It is our responsibility as parents to "educate" our

kids. We cannot fully rely on the educational system as their only means as they prepare for success and overcoming challenges. Sometimes our role as re-educator is unpopular with our kids. They would prefer we be their friend instead of their parent. I work with so many parents that want to be friends with their teens but this unrealistic. Friendly, yes; but friends, no. As a parent you have to do the hard work of sometimes being the bad guy, setting guidelines and telling kids, "no" when needed. You cannot skew the boundaries with kids because kids, by nature, test limits and push boundaries. If they don't know where the lines are, they are sure to cross them. It is hard enough to parent in this day and age when there are so many outside forces influencing kids. They need to have one place where they know their role, where they fit in, and where they come for unconditional love and acceptance as well as structure, stability, and consequences: home. I work with kids all the time that actually crave some sort of structure because their home life is so unstable and there are no boundaries. Let your kids know that you are the parent. They should expect you to be Mom or Dad and recognize that you will do whatever it takes to keep them safe and healthy.

As a parent, you should always say what you mean and mean what you say. Be firm and hold your ground, but also think carefully before you blurt out a punishment that you didn't really think through. Choose your battles. Take time to celebrate with your kids too! If they do an act of kindness, help another person, or teach themselves a new skill, take time to appreciate and encourage them. Kids are capable of learning way more than we actually teach them. It would have been inconceivable forty years ago to imagine a child could use computers, let alone install a hard drive or troubleshoot software, but some kids today can do all of that and more. We shouldn't set limits for what kids can learn. We should teach them to learn as much as they want and to learn how to acquire the necessary information to do so.

I'm a firm believer in not providing lessons for kids until they prove they are committed to them. Many parents put their kids in music, dance, skiing, riding, artistic, or sports activities. This often results in a child who has no appreciation or vested interest in the activity. I have always told my kids that if they want to learn something, they need to try it out on their own first. If they are truly interested, I will allow them to take lessons. In today's day and age, you can learn just about anything on websites like YouTube! I learned how to hot-wire a golf cart for no other reason than the information was there and it was funny! (Of course, I haven't used what I learned... yet!)

Kids learn best when they teach themselves, or others. I often encourage my older kids to assist with the homework of their younger siblings. It gives them a sense of contribution while reinforcing their own skills. I always encourage them to learn new things that they are interested in and to read as often as possible.

Reading is truly the most important thing that a kid can do. Without strong reading skills, children will struggle their entire lives. The inability to read will create roadblocks to learning basic skills like making macaroni and cheese or completing job applications. I encourage my kids to read all the time and I let them read whatever they choose. They will be more inclined to become life-long readers if they love what they are reading. My son Harry used to read wrestling magazines while my oldest daughter preferred deeply touching stories about people who overcame adversity. My middle daughter Mattie prefers fictional adventures and always has her nose in a book. It is her favorite pastime and she is always telling me about the stories she reads. I really hope my kids will read THIS book! I will continue to mention my children throughout the book... that should keep them interested!

The point of this chapter is that it is up to us to educate

our kids. We cannot set limits for them. We must let them learn new things, have weekly "home school" sessions, and teach them family values. It is up to us to teach them to go out into the world and create a fulfilling life for themselves as opposed to just "working" for someone else. They may not follow the path of the entrepreneur, but we must teach them it is an option should they want it. Kids must be allowed to make mistakes and learn from them. It allows them to grow and be savvy as they learn how to handle themselves. We must also teach them the qualities of leadership and willpower so they will be strong enough to stand up for themselves and make healthy choices. Most importantly, we must be honest with our kids. If something isn't right, we owe it to them to let them know. We don't have to give them every detail, but sugar-coating the truth doesn't allow them to learn from the experience. If there are challenges in your family, disharmony in the marriage, stress due to the loss of a job, or some other traumatic situation, talk to your kids about it.

Kids can see, hear and feel the stress in a family, despite our best efforts to shield them from it. So just be honest without blowing the situation out of proportion. State facts and encourage them to be part of the solution. Encourage kids and allow them to take part. It teaches them how to be proactive and to contribute to their family or community. Never deny or underestimate a child's experience, either. If you lived in a war zone with an abusive spouse, don't deny that it ever happened. I have met people that truly think their kids "didn't hear the arguing and fighting" or notice the police at the house twice a week. When you pretend like bad stuff didn't happen, it leaves the child confused and feeling invalidated. The pain and fear they suffered as a result of listening to their parent's battle is very real and very scary. Acknowledge it and help them learn from it and move forward. Allow them to express how scared or confused they were. Talk to them about it and apologize.

As a parent, you may have recognized a moment when your child deserved an apology, but you didn't act. They deserve it as much as anyone else. Adults make mistakes too. By not owning these mistakes, we send the message that when adults "mess up," they don't have to make amends. If you were in an abusive home in the past, talk to your kids about it. Ask them for their observations of what happened and then explain the past so they are not doomed to repeat it. You would never want your child to experience abuse so don't make that a standard for your life or theirs - ever.

A life lesson in EDUCATION:

My son Harry is such a talented young man. He is an art prodigy and at 15 years young has his own business selling his art to happy customers around the country. He has had multiple gallery showings and even had a piece selected for display in an art museum. He is truly gifted, as all my children are, but this story is about Harry in particular. Harry became interested in drawing in first grade. To encourage his interest, I bought him some "Learn to Draw" books. He wanted to take some art classes, but I told him to learn to draw first. If he found he really liked it, then we could talk about lessons. Well, Harry did teach himself to draw and he proved he had a natural knack for it. He started by drawing faces from his books, eventually moving on to still life drawings. He got to be very good, but he was hungry to learn even more. Soon he was researching shading techniques on YouTube (www.youtube.com) and it took his drawings to a new level. He would literally sit for days on end, hour after hour, drawing faces. When I recognized his talents were allowing him to create art well above his age level, I starting researching art colleges. I enrolled Harry in the continuing education classes at Rhode Island School of Design (RISD) where he took classes on cartooning and drawing with pastels. He loved it; he turned out some great pieces too. Harry continued his self-education and now does graphic design, logos, drawings, skateboard and graffiti art, cartooning and much more. He is unstoppable.

He credits me with telling him, "If you want to learn something, then just go and learn it!" He loves my "why not" attitude - an approach I offer my kids when they want to try or do something new. Why not? I teach them to take risks and try new things. I remind them it doesn't matter how old they are: they can create their world and enjoy every second of it. I remind them there will always be nay-sayers or limit setters eager to steer them off course. Regardless, I want them to go out into the world and experience a meaningful, fulfilling life. They have a choice: they can live mediocre lives where they watch others enjoy passion and excitement, or they can go out there and create their own passion and excitement.

QUICK TIPS:

~Find out what your child's learning style is: auditory, visual or kinesthetic. Advocate for them with their teachers and encourage them to learn in that way.

~All kids are smart. Reassure them when they take initiative or want to think differently.

~Don't make grades the only measure of success for your child. Teach them know how to be successful at home too.

CHAPTER 8

Detachment

"When you let go of control, you are finally free of the
expectations that disappoint you and will soon find
yourself on a path where you can truly enjoy what life
has to offer: An abundance of love and happiness!"
— Heather Paris

Detachment is the art of preventing outside
influences from controlling you, your feelings,
your emotions, or behaviors. Detachment is a skill
that requires consistent practice in order to become
proficient.

Have you ever tried to control a roller coaster while
you were on it? You can strain and flail all you want,
but you will never be able to stop a roller coaster or
control which way it goes. You may, however, end up
with a broken arm, or worse for trying. So, go with the
flow! You can't control anything except yourself, the
way you feel about events, and the way you choose to

react to things. The only thing you have the ability to control is...YOU!

Detachment is a hard concept for many to grasp but once we do, our lives open up beyond what we ever thought was possible. Choosing to not allow outside influences to control us is an amazing blessing. How many times has an ex-spouse, nosy neighbor, bitchy boss, rude cashier, terrible waitress, telemarketer, or road raged driver agitated you to the point of anger or aggression? How many times have you agonized over the unmotivated teenager that doesn't perform well in school, no matter how much bribing, negotiating or discipline you dole out? Well, my friends, when you practice detachment as a way of life, these petty, little grievances become a thing of the past.

Detachment is like playing the piano; you have to repeat it daily. It must be practiced in order for you to get really good at it. But when you do, it is effortless and free flowing. You can sit back and relax while everyone else tries to micro-manage that which cannot be controlled.

So how do you do it? Well, it's kind of like giving up, only not in the "throw in the towel" kind of way. At least that's how it worked for me. One day I just became so frustrated with the illusion of control that I was subconsciously trying to maintain. As hard as I tried, I could not control my ex-husband or his rude comments. I couldn't hold a gun to my daughter's head and force her to pay attention in class and get good grades in school. I could not force others to stop making destructive choices. I gave up trying and decided on a healthier approach. I changed how I looked at things, and the meaning I attached to them. So rather than being offended by my ex-husbands rude remarks, I recognized instead that he owned those remarks and they were a reflection of his beliefs and had nothing to do with me. I realized that while I would prefer my daughter to excel in school, I need to let her find her way and recognize that grades are not the only determining factor in her happiness or success.

I would love for the people I care about to make healthier choices but they are, ultimately, their choices, and so if they choose to smoke or drink or engage in risky behavior, it is their choice. Therefore it is their consequence and not my business. I can certainly express my concern and offer advice or help if they want it, but if they don't, I must detach from their outcome. I can still love the person while disagreeing with their behavior.

I think detachment is most difficult for parents because we are responsible for our children's long term well being. We are tasked with giving support, love, and encouragement to our children. However, when we become so attached to the outcome of who they will become or what they will do, we forget they are still on their own personal journey of growth and development. This journey is a critical requirement that must be completed in order for them to blossom into unique and thinking adults. Do we simply want to create a person, or do we want to teach creativity and allow them to grow into their own person? Teach kids, set boundaries, be clear about expectations, and allow natural consequences when possible. But then, allow kids to learn, fail, start again, and truly become someone they will love to be.

My only wish for my own children is that they grow to be happy. Detachment is a very peaceful state of surrender. It is about not giving up on life or the people around you, but merely giving up on your personal expectations for others. Place goals and expectations for you but allow others to make their own decisions. I know someone who tries to control too many aspects of her husband's life. She makes his decisions, reads his mail, checks his phone, and gives him an "allowance." She essentially micro-manages most aspects of his life. They are profoundly unhappy and I suspect they won't be able to maintain this way of life forever. She is so fearful that he is going to leave her, or that he will stray (which to the best of my knowledge he has never done), that she is actually pushing him away. Her overwhelming insecurity and her attachment to what "could happen" is wrecking their relationship. I often ask people, what is worse: having a crappy relationship with a false sense of control or, a beautiful relationship in which you make each day count knowing there are no guarantees. It is our attachments that make us unhappy. Letting go is as simple as deciding to. Take a look at your reality and then decide which way to live. When you give in and let go of things in which you don't control you truly become free. Say to yourself, "What will be will be and I can handle it."

I personally like to look at what I call "realistic worse case scenarios." For example, when Madison brings home a report card with all D's and F's, I could freak out and ground her, bribe her, or punish her, or even, ridicule and scold her. However, that would be bad for her and me. Instead I could detach from the outcome; that is, give up on worrying about what the D's and F's mean and focus on reality. "Okay, Madison," I could say, "it looks like you have some real work to do if you plan on passing eleventh grade. I know you can handle it, but let me know if I can help at all."

It would not benefit either one of us if I were to focus on how I might be judged as a Mom if my kid failed a grade, what type of remarks her Dad will make about her grades, whether or not she will get into college, or longer term, how she will support herself if she doesn't have a high school diploma. The fact is that the bad grades are there. They can't be undone. By allowing her to take responsibility for them, and to feel the natural consequences (without me getting attached to all those extra disempowering thoughts), is best for everyone. Certainly, this takes practice, but it's well worth it. I learned this lessen the hard way; I wasn't always detached!

Another area we need to detach from (especially us Super Moms) is thinking we are in control of the relationships other people build. For instance, you are not in control of the relationship your husband has with his child. If he is hard on his son, despite how you feel about it, this is still his relationship and therefore, up to him to cultivate it. I hear other Moms that tell me they hate the way their spouse interacts with their kids.

"He is too hard on him," they tell me. Or, "He only cares about his grades." And even, "He never praises him for anything!" Remember, it is not up to us to tell anyone how to maintain a relationship with another person. (Unless the person is abusive; you should never tolerate abuse towards yourself or your children). Be a beacon of love and light to everyone. Set a good example of how to treat others. Smile and offer an abundance of love, patience, and understanding to your partner and trust in knowing the relationship they cultivate with their child is part of their journey and will help to prepare your child for future life events.

We should also openly communicate with our partners and let them know of any concerns we may have. If you have a great relationship with a good foundation of communication, your spouse will be much more likely to appreciate and honor what you have to say and maybe even make changes. I hope that is the case for you. But, if they don't respond this way, you must let it go and accept their choices.

I hate the fact that anyone in life has hardships or challenges. I wish life were perfect rainbows and sunshine for all, free from suffering. But it just isn't. So I detach from the pain and have faith in the belief that we all face challenges in order to prepare us for greatness. Life isn't fair but it sure is great. After all, what is the alternative? So, let go of the pain and suffering, detach from that which we don't control, and enjoy the ride!

A life lesson in DETACHMENT:

Years ago, when I married my husband (now ex-husband) Tony, I made the decision to support his career as a Naval Officer and to go where his work might take us. Our first move was to California. This meant my daughter Madison would be moving away from her father, Don, whom she rarely saw at that point. We set up plans for calls, video chats, visits, and longer summer stays. Everyone, including Don, was on board -- or so I was led to believe. In the last moments before we left, Don had gone to the courthouse and filed an emergency restraining order. He claimed I was taking her out of state without permission and had no intent to return. I was unaware of this until I went to pick her up after a visit at her Grandmother's house; the police were on the doorstep to serve me with the court order. I couldn't go anywhere near my own child for two weeks until our court appearance. I was dazed and confused and utterly distraught. I had no idea where this had come from since Don had been agreeable, and even helpful, until this point. He even helped us move our furniture, all the while holding on to this secret that he was going to take my daughter away. With our home already set up in California, and me not being able to go near my own child who had always spent the majority of her time with me, I didn't know what to do. My lawyer suggested I just do what the court said: stay away and wait for my day in court.

Eventually, the restraining order was dropped. However, the judge allowed Madison to stay with her father in Rhode Island since he had already enrolled her in Kindergarten without me knowing. The judge then set a future court date for a custody hearing. I headed to California without my child, and later flew back to Rhode Island for court only to find out the date was pushed forward by another month. When that month expired, I hopped on another plane, only to find out the court date had again been delayed. Months passed before the judge finally heard our case. At that point, after months and months of her being with her father, the judge granted us joint custody. He said that since she was already enrolled in school and had residency with her father in Rhode Island, she was to remain with him, and when I came back to the state permanently, she was to reside with me. I lost it.

Despite these seemingly unbearable circumstances, I believed in justice and that it would all work out. I felt I had waited patiently and done all the right things but the pressure was mounting. My youngest child Harry was missing his big sister and I had a $10,000 dollar lawyer tab that was beyond my means. I went back to California without Madison and for the next year lived a very sad existence. The only joy I found was in my son Harry and I worked hard to enjoy every moment with him. I often found myself holding him tightly because I was suffering the "loss" of Madison.

I constantly berated myself with absurd questions. What kind of Mother was I to have my own child living apart from me? What would people think of me? Why would any court take my baby away and hand her over to a man that barely was a parent to her; a man that spent countless stays in drug and alcohol rehab and could barely function due to his addictions? How could I possibly live without my daughter with me? I allowed myself to writhe in pain and anguish. I began taking prescription anti-depressants to take the edge off just enough that I could get through almost a whole day without crying (as long as nobody talked to me about the situation). My husband Tony tried to be supportive, but he just didn't know what to do. My resentment toward him grew. After all, it was his career, which I had agreed to follow, that brought us clear across the country and away from my daughter.

Fast forward about seven years: My third child Carrie Sue was about six or so and I was separated from Tony, living back in Rhode Island. Madison was back with me and doing great, but I still had not gotten over the pain of that ordeal.

I had stopped taking medication long ago, had taken responsibility for my own choices, and was now moving forward in a healthy manner. Then, one day I had a memory of a time when I had visited Madison in Rhode

Island after flying in from California. I remembered going to her horse show. She was so tiny on that big horse, and while she was riding she stopped her horse in the middle of the ring and yelled at the top of her little voice, "I LOVE YOU MOMMY!" The memory of her yelling so proudly to me makes me cry, just as I did that day. It suddenly hit me that I had been more concerned about trying to control what others thought of me rather than focusing on my actual relationship with Madison. It occurred to me that no matter where we were in the world, I was still her mother and she was still my daughter, and the relationship I cultivated with her was far more important than the circumstances surrounding us. Oh my God, it hit me so hard. And when it did, I completely detached from the pain of that entire courtroom ordeal and the many years of sadness just melted away. I realized that I was a good Mom and despite our previous separation, I gave Madison all the time and love I could, even when we were apart. We talked daily and I participated in her schoolwork over the phone. I had sent presents and fun care packages and remained extremely present in her life during that period. I was beyond sad at that time, but I never let it affect my relationship with her. That is why we are still so close today. I learned that when you let go of what you have no control over and accept reality as it is, you can focus on what is truly important; the love and light that you can choose to give in all circumstances.

QUICK TIPS:
~When trying to detach, remember these tips:
- breathe deep
- focus on the positive
- ask yourself if the situation is within your control.

~Add positive thoughts to undesirable circumstances. For example, "I PREFER that things go my way, but I can handle it." Or, "I would PREFER not to get cut off when driving but it is really not that big of a deal and doesn't affect who I am."

~Life isn't just about you. We are all in it together. We need to respect the fact that other people need to learn and experience life and lessons in their own time and in their own way.

CHAPTER 9

Health/Wellness

"Take care of your body and your mind will follow."
— Heather Paris

The ability to completely take care of your body, mind, and spirit is the essence of health and wellness.

Everyone needs to take care of his or her physical body by eating healthy, getting enough rest, relaxing when necessary, and finding a comfortable level of physical activity. Consider massages and meditation to alleviate stress. Ensure proper digestive health by avoiding chemicals and toxins and drinking lots of water. Practice proper dental hygiene and take good care of your hair and nails. Last, but certainly not least, find the joy in physical touch. It is nearly impossible to feel sad or down when your body feels amazing!

"Spring clean" your mental state with positive people.

Surround yourself with those who are inspiring and uplifting. Dump the "Debbie Downers" and "Becky Backstabbers" and set a new standard for yourself. Clear your mind and thoughts with some quiet time and meditation. Mental clarity is a beautiful thing!

Most of us do not get adequate vitamins and minerals each day via the food that we eat. The funny thing about the world in which we live is that obesity is so prevalent, yet most people who are overweight are actually under nourished because they are not eating enough of the right types of foods. You should take vitamin supplements everyday. We also avoid pharmaceuticals as much as possible. I don't even like to take an ibuprofen. I prefer to be completely drug free. There are so many natural cures, especially food cures, for most ailments. You can also find homeopathic medicines in your grocery stores. I also love holistic healers; I utilize chiropractors, acupuncturists, and massage therapists. I believe most ailments and diseases can be treated (or even prevented) without polluting your body with drugs. Start eating healthy and participate in some form of daily exercise in order to create a healthier body today.

Eat food the way it is born -- fresh! Choose foods from the garden or from the produce section at the grocery store. Food is healthier in its natural state when it is still fresh and unprocessed. Fill your kitchen with whole food choices for your family. Avoid making your fridge a morgue by loading it with meat and processed foods. Avoid pesticides and genetically modified products by choosing organic options if they are available in your area, as well.

Exercise is GREAT for the body and mind! In my opinion, every person should get at least 30 minutes per day of exercise. This is great for your overall health and well-being. What is the very best type of exercise to do??? Answer: The exercise that you will consistently do! Set yourself up for success by participating in exercises that you enjoy. Sex, housework, jogging, playing with the kids, walking the dog, bike riding, skating: these are all forms of physical exercise that can be done daily to raise your heart rate. (Did you hear that? You HAVE to have sex because it is good exercise!)

Also, consuming enough water is essential to health. Drink half your body weight in ounces each day. For instance, if you weigh 150 pounds, drink 75 ounces of water daily. Water is life!

Taking care of your body is the most important thing you can do, yet somehow, we tend to forget that. Without your health nothing else will matter. Don't wait until a disease forces you to think about taking care of yourself; do it now. Staying healthy and fit also sets a great example for your kids. In a country where childhood obesity is out of control, we owe it to our children to teach them to eat healthy and take care of their bodies. It is our responsibility to provide healthy meals as we encourage them to become physically active. As we encourage them to stay physically healthy, we also need to be cognizant of their mental health as well.

Kids need to discharge their negative emotions and feelings just as much as grown ups. We should offer them time daily to talk about anything that is on their mind. At my house, we do this around the dinner table each night. We take turns talking about our day and the kids love it when it is their turn and everyone has to sit and listen to them. They love the spotlight. It gives me such a great feeling too, because the kids love hearing about my day as well. I talk to them about the children I work with and share any revelations they may have had (without giving them names or other confidential information). When I tell them about an underprivileged young person, we talk about what we can do to help. My kids have always been involved in our household philanthropic efforts. They have helped me buy, wrap, and deliver presents, clothes, blankets, and coats to homeless shelters. We have anonymously sent Christmas gifts in the mail and we often make cards for sick kids in the hospital. There is nothing better for your child's mental state than to help another kid in need. It gives them an opportunity to contribute beyond themselves and it offers them the chance to really appreciate and be grateful for what they have. A grateful heart makes for a healthy mind!

I personally love meditation for stress relief and for overall well-being. Meditation calms, soothes, relaxes and helps provide clarity. Many of us maintain busy lifestyles today and it is imperative that we take time out to rest our minds and slow down. Our bodies need time to relax and replenish so they stay will strong and can fight germs and provide optimal health and energy.

One of the physical activities I absolutely love is rebounding (jumping on a small trampoline). It is great exercise and it assists the lymphatic system in carrying waste from your body. Even if you do it for only five minutes a day, do it! Speaking of waste, (yes, I am going to do it, I am going to mention poop), I can't tell you how many people go days without pooping; this is so completely unhealthy. People should be pooping daily and it should be easy. If you are straining during a bowel movement then you are not doing something right. Eat plenty of fiber and vegetables and drink enough water each day and you will be pooping in no time! I am a vegetarian and I highly recommend not eating meat proteins. There are so many reasons why a vegetarian diet is healthier, but I will let you do your own research.

People get all crazy when you try and take their meat away and I am not going to try and force you to do that. But I will suggest that you watch the movie Forks over Knives. If nothing else, try working a few vegetarian recipes into your weekly meals.

Okay, that's it on vegetarianism - I promise!

A life lesson in HEALTH and WELLNESS:

As a child, I had severe asthma and allergies. I was always on some sort of medication, required to do regular breathing treatments, and had to submit to skin tests every few months in order to monitor my allergies. I was in and out of the hospital the first couple years of life and my parents were always worried. They did everything in their power to keep me well, including staying up all night long to walk with me in their arms and working several jobs to pay the medical bills. They must have been exhausted. I cannot even imagine the fear they must have felt. My father joined the Army shortly thereafter. The armed forces offered free medical services and that meant everything to them!

I don't think my parents ever really stopped worrying about my health. Throughout my entire childhood they took me to the doctor regularly in an effort to combat the symptoms of my afflictions. I spent my entire childhood on asthma and allergy medications until I was in 7th grade. That was the year when teachers contacted my parents to schedule a parent/ teacher conference because I was "flaking out" in school (more than usual). The teachers asked my parents if I was using illegal drugs. Naturally, my parents were insulted by this accusation. The teachers reported that I just didn't seem to "be there" and was napping in class. My parents stormed out of the school, completely affronted by the fact that the teachers would accuse their child of being doped up.

In an effort to figure out what might be wrong with me, they brought me to a child psychologist. My father took me to my first and only appointment. After the receptionist greeted us she looked at me, looked back and him and asked, "Is this session for you and your wife?"

"This is my daughter!" he said forcefully.

I thought that was the funniest thing ever, but my dad didn't find it nearly as humorous.

In we went to see the psychologist and after taking a good look at him, I was even more amused. I don't really remember a word he said, but the moment we got in the office I noticed he had two different colored socks on: one green and one red. When you are thirteen, that's funny stuff! As we began the session, I watched carefully as he took a pipe and cleaning tools out of his drawer. He pulled the garbage can toward him, leaned over it and carefully began to clean his pipe. He seemed to do a thorough job too. I figure it must have taken him at least thirty minutes. When he was finished, he packed it full of tobacco and lit it. Then, as the smoke circled my face, he leaned toward me and said, "Do you mind if I smoke?"

I began laughing uncontrollably because I thought it was so funny that he would go through all of the effort of cleaning, packing, and lighting the pipe, only to ask us (after the fact) if we minded if he smoked. I couldn't stop laughing and I'm sure my Dad was ticked off by my inappropriate behavior!

After the comedy of the pipe and some further discussion, the psychologist said he didn't see anything wrong with me. He felt that my behavior seemed completely age appropriate and suggested my parents look more closely at the medications I was on. They followed his advice and discovered, I was completely doped up on asthma medication. Apparently the time for a lower dosage had long passed and my erratic behavior was a symptom of my body reacting to being over medicated. Wow!

My parents carefully weaned me off of the medication until I was able to take it only as needed. I still had some issues with asthma but they were completely manageable with rescue inhalers. I was much better in school too, and no longer fell asleep or got accused of being a drug user.

I will never forget that experience. I was completely confused and had no idea I was "flaking out." It made me feel bad to think my teachers thought I was abusing drugs. I thank my parents for staying on top of things and making sure to do everything possible to ensure that I was healthy. They knew their kid and they knew I would never use drugs. I guess this is why now as an adult I am against the use of pharmaceuticals in general. I know there are times when you can't avoid it, but I personally try really hard never to use prescription drugs. I encourage everyone to think about the changes they can make in their diets and lifestyles to decrease the amount of drugs they take and increase the amount of energy and happiness they feel.

QUICK TIPS:
~Eat healthy. Try to avoid or, at least, limit meats and eat plenty of fresh vegetables and fruit.
~Drink half your body weight in ounces of water daily.
~Exercise at least 20-30 minutes per day.
~Avoid medications when possible.
~Meditate and get plenty of rest.

CHAPTER 10

Death

"We are all drops of water. When you place a single drop into the ocean it is no longer just one drop, it becomes part of an entire ocean; the ocean is much larger than a drop but it is still water."

— Heather Paris

I believe that death is not the end but is merely a transformation into a different state of existence. It is one of the biggest fears that we, as a people, share. We are afraid to no longer exist and the biggest reason for this is because we don't have a realistic view of death. We think we will live forever. Because of this, when we do suffer a loss, it feels so unjust and overwhelming. We never want to face the fact that death is a part of life. Once we are able to accept that each moment is a gift and nothing is guaranteed in life, we can have a healthier outlook on one of the things that every human on earth will have to deal with at some point. We often speak of death in whispers, like it is cursed and will "get us" if we acknowledge it. We tip toe around the topic because nobody is completely certain what happens after death. We don't teach our kids about death because it is too gloomy or macabre. I am here to tell you that no one cheats death and nobody whispers himself or herself away from the truth. There is good news; you can have a healthier outlook and free yourself from the fear.

I am not entirely sure how I got my views on death. I suppose they were acquired through my life experiences; my parents never actually had any formal conversations with me about death or dying. In retrospect, they did seem to have a pretty healthy outlook on death and I "learned" from their actions.

Rather than allowing our children to learn from our cues, we should have discussions about mortality with them. This is especially true of teens who often believe they are indestructible. They should learn to not participate in destructive activities in their lives. There are no "do overs" and we don't get second chances. Dead is dead. Our kids should learn that every single moment we have with the people we care about is a gift - not a guarantee. At any moment, our life, or a loved one's life, can stop.

I have a friend who asked me recently how she could create a compelling future for a loved one that had cancer.

I told her. "First, I would stop trying to find a 'compelling future' for them. The fact is they may not have one, and ignoring that makes them feel like their fears are invalid. I am all about being positive and realistic. Live in each moment. There is no future, not for any single person on earth. There is only this moment right now. A healthy person has no more guarantees than a person with cancer. I would encourage them to find joy in things they can enjoy 'right now' like: watching funny movies, listening to favorite music choices, talking with friends, or spending time with children. Focus on what you can do today, even if it means watching a bunch of comedy routines while you sit through a chemotherapy treatment. Everyone's life is full of unknowns and having them believe their unknowns are exclusive just adds to the burden. Help them focus on the here and now. Be realistic. For example they might say, "Cancer sucks and I am afraid, but I will do what I can to get through this and I know that the future is guaranteed to no one. I will make the most of what I have now."

My friend appreciated my outlook and was grateful that I took the time to help her see things differently. You need to remember that life is short. You owe it to yourself to suck every last little moment out of it; enjoy and savor the magic moments while you have them and always make time for the people we care about.

I have been diagnosed and successfully treated for cervical cancer. This experience helped me gain a perspective that I am grateful for. I certainly wouldn't wish this horrible disease on anyone, but it can be a defining event that actually makes us appreciate life much more! It is important to realize that detachment is the key during these types of life challenges.

Live a good life that people will honor and create a legacy that others will remember you for. Death comes to those who make the most of their life and choose to give back to the world, just as it comes to people who are abusive, self serving, or choose to use their life to harm others. How do you want to be remembered? Do you want people to celebrate you or breathe a sigh of relief when you are gone? You are responsible for how you live your life. The way you treated others is what people will remember after you are gone.

When you experience a loss of a loved one, you should celebrate their life. You should remember the good and be grateful for the time you had with them. The loss of a loved one will always make you feel sad, but if you truly live with passion and enjoy the moments you have with people, you will be at peace, knowing your time together was memorable and fulfilling.

Millions find comfort in religion or spirituality after a loss. My personal belief is that you are made of energy, an energy that can neither be created nor destroyed. Once you die, you become part of an Universal energy that surrounds us all. (Some say God, I say Universe.) Remember, once you die, you become like that drop of water in the ocean, no longer a single drop but part of something much bigger.

I don't believe in heaven or hell. I don't believe that some people get preference while others get torture. I don't believe in earthly rituals to ensure your spot in an afterlife. I simply believe that when you die, your energy transfers into the Universal energy and you don't exist in the same way anymore. No ghosts, no limbo, no devils or angels, no harps and clouds, or pearly gates. You just stop living and your energy becomes part of the whole. I agree with the existentialist, Osho, who said, "The real question is not whether life exists after death. The real question is whether you are alive before death."

A life lesson in DEATH:

Several years ago my best friend Blake died. He and I were born only thirteen days apart. We were in our early 30s when he stopped living and joined the Universe.

Blake was a great guy. He was a real character and often went overboard with his humor but he never stopped being a true friend. He was such a jokester and just loved to torture me. One night he called me on the phone and asked what I was doing. He made small talk, luring me into comfortable conversation. All the while, he was standing outside my dining room window waiting to scare the crap out of me…and he did! After a few minutes of us yapping, I got up and walked through the dining room. He had pressed himself up against the dark glass and his reflection nearly gave me a heart attack! He laughed his ass off. That was his kind of humor! Sometimes he was raunchy and inappropriate but I loved him. We had been friends since 9th grade and had gone through a lot together. He even confided in me, "coming out" about his homosexuality, which was not as acceptable in the early 90s as it is today.

Blake and I were also friends with Carrie; the three of us didn't do much of anything without one another. Even as adults, we ALWAYS told each other everything! Sometimes, too much… The three of us would stay on the phone for hours each night. Carrie and I had a crafting business together, so we would talk while crafting and Blake would keep us laughing with his special brand of humor. What would we have done without three-way calling?

There was a point when we were literally on the phone with each other every single night for up to 6 hours at a time. We would sit, talk, laugh, craft and carry on and on. We often talked about death and the afterlife and were convinced there was a "special place" for the three of us! My motto at the time was "You're gonna DIE, so why not LIVE!" I often talked about the need for us to live with passion because life was not guaranteed to anyone. When Blake wanted to consider a new business, I told him, "Just do it! You're going to die someday. Knowing that, why would you ever put anything off?" These proved to be prophetic words.

Our daily phone calls often lasted well into the early morning hours and continued for quite some time. I am not really sure how any of our spouses put up with us, but the bond we all had was undeniable. I believe it was exactly what we all needed at that time and am grateful for this gift.

The day before Blake died, the three of us planned to get together and shop. Carrie was unable to make it, so it was just Blake and me. I met him after work and we went to lunch and talked for hours. Afterwards, we walked through the mall and talked and laughed some more. Blake suggested we go into one of the jewelry stores and pretend to be an engaged couple. He hatched a plan in which we would pretend to buy the most expensive diamond in the store only to get in a loud fight and break-up in front of the sales girl just before she closed her biggest sale ever. (I told you he was a real character!) We didn't end up doing it because I was too concerned about the salesgirls feelings, but we laughed about it for a very long time afterwards.

We walked back to his place of employment in the mall and he teased me about my "ugly purse." I hugged him and thanked him for the day, telling him I would see him later. I went home, never thinking for a second that this would be the last time I saw him. Later that evening the phone rang. My husband, at the time, said, "It's Blake. Do you want me to answer it?"

"No," I said. "I spent the whole day with him. I'm tired. I'll call him in the morning."

The next morning the phone rang early. It was Carrie. I could barely understand her as she gasped and cried, "Blake is dead!"

I couldn't understand what she was saying. I tried to calm her down, but she just kept saying that Blake was dead. I thought for sure it was another one of his jokes. It seemed like something he would put Carrie up to. Unfortunately, I was wrong. I asked her to tell me everything. She said she called him and his brother answered. He told her he was at the hospital and that Blake was dead. I was stunned. I told Carrie I would find out the truth. I hung up and immediately called Blake's family. They confirmed; he was gone.

I later learned he had gotten up that morning to

shower and get ready for work. Just before he stepped into the shower, he dropped dead from a brain aneurism. There was no warning. He was a healthy guy, he never did drugs, didn't drink alcohol, he never even got sick; now, he was dead.

I called Carrie back and confirmed the worst. I felt so sad, but I called Blake's life partner Chris and asked him what I could do. I just wanted to help. Weeks later, Chris let me come over and help him go through Blake's things. We laughed and cried as we talked about how much we loved Blake and how he loved to torture us. Chris and I became close and it felt so great to be able to help him through his loss. I knew Blake would have been grateful.

Through this all, I never got angry, I was never in denial, and I never bargained. I felt sad that our time was done but I was eternally grateful for the time we shared. I was grateful I was with him for a part of his last day on earth, and I will always be grateful for the memories I have.

I think my healthy outlook on death helped me get through that difficult time. I wish everyone could see death as a part of life and work to live life to the fullest, instead of fearing their death. Never miss an opportunity to help someone or tell someone you love them. And in times of death, let go of your own pain and be a source of joy for others.

QUICK TIPS:

~Talk to your kids about death and share your beliefs about what happens afterward with them.

~Live a good life filled with compassion and caring for others.

~When death occurs, focus on how you can help or what you can give.

~Cherish happy memories and be grateful for the time you had.

~Live a life of gratitude and take nothing or no one for granted.

CHAPTER 11:

Rediscovering Innocence

"It is never too late to set a new standard
of what you find acceptable."
— Heather Paris

What does it mean to rediscover your innocence? For me, it's about taking a step back, re-evaluating your choices and setting a new standard for what you find acceptable! It offers the chance to remember old joys and to re-establish a new standard for what you accept in your life.

I recently worked with a teenager that had already engaged in sexual activities with multiple partners at her young age of fourteen. At the time we spoke, she was involved in a relationship with an abusive boyfriend. I told her it was not too late to start over and set a new standard. She could just stop making poor choices and having sexual relationships that were meaningless. I told her she should save herself for someone when she became an adult in a committed relationship. We talked for quite some time, and she revealed to me that she was very unhappy with the choices she had made. She told me she was worried that if she ever married, she would not want to have sex with her husband because she had already been with so many boys with whom the experiences had been less than stellar. I told her if she gave her body, heart and mind time to heal, she would be able to grow into a responsible adult who would be able to enjoy a healthy and happy relationship. She needed to allow herself to be a 14-year-old girl again and embrace age appropriate behaviors, while giving up the things she thought made her mature (sex). I recommended she go to a movie, visit the library, or explore a nearby museum. I suggested she spend time at the mall with her girlfriends, or doing her hair and nails. I encouraged her to do all the things 14-year-old girls like to do. By implementing age appropriate behaviors, as opposed to spending all of her time with her boyfriend, she would be able to rediscover herself and enjoy her youthfulness. She did make these changes, and it gave her an entirely new perspective on life.

She dumped her abusive boyfriend and reconnected with her family, whom had been concerned for her safety. She apologized to teachers, friends and everyone else she felt she had wronged. She made a decision to dedicate her time to living a much healthier life! I am so proud of her and grateful that she was able to find her innocence again. She smiled and giggled more, found new girl friends, and really embraced her age instead of trying to grow up too fast.

When I was young, cell phones didn't exist. I was very much part of an era where staying at home in order to receive an important phone call was the norm. We wrote letters, instead of e-mails, and waited weeks for a response. Today, it seems kids wait for nothing. And if they feel like they have to wait for something, they become extremely frustrated. Our society possesses the misconceived notion that results are instantaneous. Because of this, we have lost sight of the excitement that comes with anticipation. We no longer know what it's like to appreciate anything because we don't have to wait for results.

We used to wait to buy things until we had the money too. Nowadays, many of us use credit to purchase whatever we want and worry about paying for it later. I truly believe our society has suffered some because of this. It makes me sad to see so many young, impatient people that want everything right now. What's worse is that they want to grow up too fast too. As parents, friends, neighbors, grandparents, and a society as a whole, we need to take the time to teach our kids that growing up too fast holds no benefits. They must understand that it's fun to be a kid as we teach them to enjoy all the wonderment that childhood offers. If that means taking away their cell phone, iPad, laptop, TV, or any other distracting device, then do so!

Make FAMILY the priority and set limits for the use of electronics. In our home, we don't have television service. We do allow the kids to watch movies but we have no cable or satellite. Additionally, we don't allow any television viewing during the school week at all. I am not the type to blame television for all the evils of the world but the fact is, what you put in is what you give out. If you are watching crap all the time, you cannot possibly be enhancing yourself in any way. Kids today watch shows that depict other kids lying, cheating, drinking, doing drugs, having sex, and outwitting their parents. I feel that when kids watch this kind of content, it desensitizes them. They get the impression that the behaviors they see on TV represent how other kids and families function. Television (including "reality TV") does not portray a realistic picture of how life truly is. As a result of allowing this unrealistic programming, I believe we are setting our kids up for failure. The glorification of bad behavior has no positive influences on children in any way and I find it difficult to imagine that anyone could consider this entertaining.

Of course, not all television is bad. There are plenty of educational channels that include my favorite genre: documentaries. We also love Ted.com. Not only is it educational, it offers uplifting and innovative "talks" that inspire everyone to achieve greatness.

Our kids do have standard cell phones (without data plans or Internet) but they are not allowed at the dinner table or during conversations. In fact, the only reason they really have a mobile phone is because I enjoy peace of mind that comes with being able to reach them at any time.

The computer has limits on it as well. They each get an allotted amount of time to be "online." They may use the computer as much as they want for research, typing, photo editing, or anything else that enables them to rely upon their own creativity and expand their imagination. The older kids have Facebook and Twitter accounts but we are "friends" with them so we can see what they are posting. We also have a "if you won't say it to your grandparents then don't post it online" policy.

I encourage you to kick the kids outside daily. Some of my kids would never leave the house if they didn't have to, so I make them go outside to get some fresh air and exercise. We live in a country setting with several acres of land. We have lots of fun, wooded areas, and waterfront, which gives them plenty of places to explore. We have a big trampoline, ATVs, a huge hill for climbing, dogs, chickens, goats, and plenty of other outdoor toys. In fact, if you name it, we've probably got it. There is absolutely no reason why they shouldn't be outdoors and enjoying some sunshine. When we lived in the suburbs, our yard was much smaller but there was still enough room for them to play outside and engage in activities with the other neighborhood kids.

If you have limited yard space, take your children to the park or nearby school playground. Do whatever it takes to get them out so they can discover all of the joys of nature. It's good for their health and a wonderful way to teach them how to enjoy the pleasures of being young.

Another way to maintain family bonds is to enjoy a daily meal together. Each night at my house we sit at the table together and share a family dinner. It doesn't have to be anything formal or fancy, but the idea is to come together and share the details of our day. Too many families are not eating together anymore. We need to spend time together daily to reconnect and ensure the family bond stays strong. That bond is strengthened by spending time together, sharing stories, discussing challenges, and engaging in each others lives.

A life lesson in REDISCOVERING INNOCENCE:

When I was younger I used to love to go into the woods and explore. I would get on my bike after breakfast and disappear for the entire day. My curfew was, officially, when the streetlights came on. Until then, my friends and I would go traipsing through the woods, exploring every inch. We found abandoned, run-down homes and shacks, dilapidated cars, and even an old one-room schoolhouse that still had books and other remnants of a day when single classrooms educated all ages at once. We pretended to be tight-rope walkers as we tiptoed along fallen trees that lay precariously over ravines and streams. We imagined we were Tarzan as we swung from the vines hanging in the woods. We would yell and scream and laugh and run and jump and just carry on. It was so much fun; I loved those days. Then, one day, something happened…

I turned sixteen! It was all over from there. As soon as I possibly could, I got my driver's permit, and soon thereafter, my license. To me, that license meant complete freedom. (I would discover later that I had much more freedom as a care free child than I did as a young adult with responsibilities). Once I learned how to drive, in an act of ultimate "defiance," I threw my bike off the back deck, never to ride it again. To me, the act of launching my bike was a major milestone; an act that defined the end of an era and the beginning of new one; this was my grown up, "driving" life!

My aunt was kind enough to buy me my first car: a Dodge Colt, light blue in color, with a hatchback body style. It looked good, but I quickly learned it wouldn't run until I filled the gas tank. That's when I realized my new adult driving life came with many responsibilities that I had not previously considered. Among those were paying for gas and auto insurance. I had already worked, babysitting on weekends and serving as a camp counselor in the summers, but now it was becoming clear that it was time for a "real" job, making real money! I started working at Burger King when I was sixteen, working after school and on weekends. I continued to work there after I graduated high school and picked up a second job at the youth center as well. I look back now and wonder why I wanted to "grow up" and get a job so bad. Being an adult is great but being a kid was so much more fun! In hindsight, I realize that I often overcomplicated the simplicity of childhood. I often share stories with my kids about my childhood in hopes that they will know that this is the "time of their lives". They should take advantage of their youth and enjoy it. I tell them they should relax and take their time to grow and always appreciate how much freedom they have. I hope they enjoy it while they can!

QUICK TIPS:

~Set a new standard for what you find acceptable for yourself.

~It is never too late to make a change or start again.

~Be careful not to desensitize yourself to things you know may be unhealthy for you.

~Embrace family.

CHAPTER 12:

Kindness/Compassion/Giving

"Always give beyond yourself. Do things to help others. Make a difference in another's life. Love beyond limits. Life is about what you give!"
— Heather Paris

Kindness, compassion, and giving are the things that can make you happiest. You should always take the opportunity to do something for someone, no matter how small that something seems to be. Always give beyond yourself. Donate your time, energy, and resources. Something as simple as offering a sympathetic ear can mean the world to someone in need of a sounding board. We all have something to give. When you give, you live. Kindness is essential to a happy life. I believe, at our core, we are created as kind, loving creatures. We often grow cynical or crabby through circumstance, but that is not who you start out as. Always be kind to everyone and everything.

Kindness is a reflection of self. If you put kindness into the Universe, you will feel kindness in return.

Last winter I was driving through the parking lot of a shopping plaza when I noticed a man in a wheelchair at the bottom of an icy hill. He was struggling desperately to wheel himself up. I pulled over near the hill and got out of my car to help the man. I announced myself as I walked up behind him so as not to startle him.

"I'm okay, I can do it," he shouted when he saw me.

As I got closer to him I noticed he had only one leg. He continued to try and push himself upward; the wheels on the chair just kept on spinning.

"Please sir, let me help," I said. I took the handles on the back of his chair, leaned forward and pushed him up the icy hill. Once we reached the top I asked him if he was okay. He indicated he just needed to get across the street and that he could handle it from here. He thanked me for my help and went happily on his way. I left him safely at his destination, and that left me feeling good. I could have driven right past him, but I would have missed a valuable opportunity to provide kindness to another person. And who knows how long he may have been stuck there trying to get up the hill.

Being compassionate to those who are suffering is a gift to you as much as it is to them. You should be equally compassionate with yourself, allowing you to make mistakes without beating yourself up and damaging your self-worth. Compassion can come in the form of an understanding smile, a listening ear, a hug, a gentle nod, or a pat on the back. Compassion is when you empathize with someone else and what they are feeling. Even if you can't empathize, you can put your own feelings or thoughts on hold long enough to validate what the other person is feeling. Compassion is a skill that requires the absence of ego and the abundance of heart.

I have always considered myself a philanthropist. In fact, I'm happiest when I feel like I am giving to the world in some way. Sometimes I do it by volunteering, other times through random acts of kindness. More than once, I have taken children that are in need into our home. In the past couple of years I have opened my home to three different teenagers, two of which were homeless and one who was displaced because he was gay. I believe in doing whatever you can to help others and to make the Universe a better place. Life provides so many opportunities to do good things. These opportunities for kindness, compassion, and generosity are everywhere; you only need keep your eyes and heart open to find them. If you see someone who looks confused, ask if you can help him or her. If you see someone struggling to reach something in the store, step up and grab it for them. If you see an elderly person trying to make her way somewhere, lend a hand. When you see a child in need, reach out. Even if you can't take them into your home, you could be a mentor or a good example for them. Take some food to a family in need. Send Christmas presents to a family that can't afford them. Leave change on the ground for someone to find. Whatever you do, you will feel great knowing you are making a difference and helping someone out.

A life lesson in KINDNESS/ COMPASSION/ GIVING:

I was the kid who always brought home stray pets and kids. It seems it has always been engrained within me to try and save the world, one person at a time. When I was a 4th grader still living in Germany, I actually "stole" another child in an effort to help them out! During lunch we had to ride the bus home to eat and then ride it back to school again when we were done. My best friend at the time was Edie. I loved her. She had the coolest Afro and it was huge! (It was the 70s, after all.) We spent every moment together at school and I was like a mother hen to her, sticking up for her and protecting her. Somehow, I determined she needed help or guidance although, I cannot remember why. This much I do remember; One day she told me she didn't have anything to eat at home and so she would come back to school hungry. Well, in my few years on the earth at that time, there was one thing I did know – and that was that no child should ever go hungry. I told her I would take care of everything and told her to stick by my side. At lunchtime I smuggled her onto my bus and brought her home with me. Terrorism was a problem at that time and I can't even imagine how her mother must have felt when her daughter didn't come home from school when she was supposed to. In fact, we only had to take the bus home for lunch because terrorists had blown up the club next to our school which left our lunchroom damaged. We didn't even have phones in our military housing so Edie couldn't call home to notify her parents.

When I walked into the house my mother flipped her lid.

"Who is this?" she demanded. "Where did she come from? What class is she in? What bus was she supposed to take? Why did you bring her home?"

My Mom continued to shout at Edie and me, but I could barely understand her, she was so angry. She was clearly concerned for Edie's parents, as well as upset that I had "kidnapped" a fellow student. I explained that Edie was going to have to live with us now because she wasn't going to be fed at her house and that was simply not acceptable. My mother let me know that taking kids home from school was not acceptable. She told us to sit down and eat our lunch so she could march us right back to the bus. Before sending us on our way, she sternly reminded me that I was to allow Edie to go home on her own bus and was never to smuggle another kid home again!

I never did find out if poor Edie was really in need or what happened after I took her home for lunch that day. I assume it all worked out because the next day she was back at school like nothing ever happened. Although we were not allowed to hang out anymore, we were still best friends until the day her dad got transferred to another base. I never saw or heard from her again but I never forgot my friend.

They say people come into your life for a reason, a season, or a lifetime. I hope I provided her with something she can always keep with her, even if it's just knowing people care. Maybe Edie came into my life to help me create a legacy of helping others. Either way, I am grateful for knowing her.

QUICK TIPS:

~Always be kind, even when others are not kind to you.

~You may never know what another is going through but you can always show them compassion and let them know they are not alone.

~Give, give, and give. It feels amazing and makes life enjoyable for everyone involved!

~Kindness, compassion, and giving create happiness.

CHAPTER 13:

Positivity

"I would rather be wide-eyed and full of smiles,
knowing that it will all work out, rather than feeling
upset by the world which I don't control."
— Heather Paris

Positivity is the ability to believe the best will emerge from every situation, even if you are not sure how. Being positive takes practice; do, in order to become! You can always see things in a positive way or a negative way, so why not choose the positive way? You have to commit to being positive daily and really make an effort. Every time you are inclined to see the bad in a situation, resist and find the good! Even if the good is, "I am not sure how this will play out, but I trust it WILL work out for the best!"

Being positive and upbeat makes life more fun and it makes other people more comfortable around you. I've said it before and I'll say it again: nobody likes to hang around a Debbie Downer. She steals people's energy and it can be very draining. Would you rather attract others or push them away?

Look at changing your outlook in this way: If you don't like the rain, at least acknowledge how vital the rain is for our plants, grass, livestock, and for the overall health of the planet. Then, grab an umbrella and put on a smile! You don't have to LIKE everything, but you don't have to complain about what you don't like either. Be positive and positive things will come your way.

I have often had people say to me, "Of course you're always happy and positive... Your life is perfect!" Well guess what? It IS perfect but only because I choose to see it that way! I have plenty of challenges (notice I don't say problems) and "bad things" happen but I accept these as part of the bigger picture. Those undesirable events make me appreciate the "good things" all that much more. I believe you wouldn't appreciate the sweetness of life if you didn't have to taste the bitter parts from time to time. I accept that challenges are part of life. They make me stronger and wiser as I continue to focus on what is positive and uplifting.

Adopt the phrase, "It will all work out." Things always work out the way they are supposed to and if you continue to tell yourself that, you will adopt a positive mindset that will help you get through tough times. Bear this in mind: never once has a problem been so big that the entire world has ended as a result. People live and people die. People get hurt and end up heartbroken. However, those same people can always move forward from the hurt and learn from it. If you have faith that things will work out, if you remind yourself that everything has worked out so far, and if you tell yourself, "This is challenging but I can handle it," you will be able to accept those things you have no control over.

Instead of greeting people with the traditional "How are you?" start instead with asking them, "So, what's good?" People will be more inclined to tell you something positive they have going, as opposed to anything else. People like other positive people. They will remember how you made them feel over anything else. When someone asks you how your day was, do you whine and complain about all the atrocities of the day or do you focus on the great things that have happened in your life today?

Adapt to situations and make the most of it. Life, events and people are always changing. Learn to be flexible and go with the flow. Nobody wants to hear you complain about how far away from the store entrance you had to park, or how complicated the new software you struggle with at the office is, or how the store was out of your favorite coffee flavor. Remain positive, stay flexible, and adjust to your environment.

Positivity also yields healthful benefits. Research proves that laughter alone does remarkable things:

- Boost your immune system
- Lower stress levels
- Decreases pain
- Burn calories
- Relaxes your muscles
- Eases anxiety
- Makes you happy
- Makes others want to be in your presence
- Defuses conflict
- Creates bonds
- Releases "feel good" endorphins

Being positive is good for you and everyone you come in contact with. Practice it until it becomes habit and enjoy all the benefits of seeing the best in every situation!

A life lesson in POSITIVITY:

Every time there is a major crisis or catastrophe in the world, people generally tend to become addicted to the news channels and focus on the negativity. However,

I prefer to focus on the positive things that emerge and give my attention to solutions when possible.

In October of 2012, Hurricane Sandy hit the East Coast of the United Stated with a vengeance; the news media wasted no time in telling everyone how horrible and devastating things were. They seemed to leave out all the stories of heroes who were stepping up and helping one another. In the aftermath of the storm, people were donating food, clothes, shelter, money, and services. Media reports of these stories seemed to be few and far between. I understand their goal is to report factual news but it seems as though they are actually just peddling fear and profiting on people's feelings of desperation and impending doom. This is one of the reasons why we don't have television service in our home.

A friend of mine, Joanne, who lives in the area hit hardest by the storm had set herself up to accept donations and generously distributed them as soon as she received them. I helped share the information about where donations could go and I also purchased Wal-Mart gift cards and donated them.

I believe there is always something you can do to help when situations arise and focusing on helping makes you feel good. You are less likely to obsess on the crisis or wallow in negativity if you are focused on helping and serving people or pets in need. This has always been my viewpoint; stay positive and focus on helping. Remember, in crisis, there are always heroes. We can either praise the heroes and help the needy or we can focus on the chaos and perpetuate the problem. Positivity is far more helpful and it is always our choice!

QUICK TIPS:
~ Be positive and you will attract positive experiences to your life.
~ People enjoy being around positive people.
~ Look for the bright side in every situation.
~ Being positive and laughing is good for your health.

CHAPTER 14:

Confidence

"I don't care who you are, what you look like,
where you are from, or what you do; you can be
as awesome as you will allow yourself to be!"
—Heather Paris

Confidence is the possession of a true belief in yourself, your beauty, your abilities, your strengths, and your self-worth. I can't say this enough; confidence is the sexiest, most powerful accessory you could ever put on. If you have trouble mustering up confidence, here is a tip: Think about a moment in your life when you felt really confident. It should be a moment when you knew your stuff or you looked amazing and knew it. Maybe you did a job really well and felt great about it. Whatever the memory is, relive it as vividly as you can in your mind. Now, stitch that moment into the lining of a "coat" that you can put on at any moment.

You may choose to wear your coat every day, or only in moments when you need extra confidence. Just picture yourself putting on that coat of confidence each time you need a little boost. Use your coat when you are feeling nervous or challenged, or when you want to make a good impression. By wrapping yourself in this "coat of confidence", you will be able to overcome any doubts or fears that may arise.

Please note: confidence is sexy as hell, so don't be surprised by the attention you get when you wear it!

A life lesson in CONFIDENCE:

I have never really lacked in confidence! I guess it was being raised by two confident parents that did it because my sister is pretty confident too. My confidence has gotten me farther in life than pretty much anything. Once I applied for a case manager position that I knew I would be amazing at, even though I didn't have the bachelors degree that it required. My friend had asked why I was even bothering to apply since I was not qualified. I told her that I was qualified, probably over qualified and so what if I didn't have the degree. I mean really... did they want someone with a piece of paper or someone who could do the job well?

I went to the interview, spoke with confidence, talked about what I would do to improve the lives of the elderly people I would be working with, and expressed that they would never find a more loyal or responsible employee. I was offered the job on the spot and my boss was amazing! He was by far the best boss I ever had. He once told me that I reminded him of his Mom, because I too was a single mother like his mother had been, I was a hard worker and I took good care of my kids. While I worked there, for about 3 years, I received an award from the Department of Elderly Affairs, I was nominated for a humanitarian award, I was hired by the New Jersey Housing authority to speak about a program I had implemented, and I was interviewed on television for the good work I was doing advocating for the elderly. I am very glad I had the confidence to apply!

I try and instill this trait in my kids, as well as the kids I work with. In today's competitive world, you need far more than a degree. People with self confidence, a good worth ethic, and dedication really stand out! You want to be the one who stands out in the crowd, take a chance, you never know until you try!

QUICK TIPS:

~ Confidence is the sexiest accessory anyone could wear.

~ Recall a positive and confident moment when you need more confidence.

~ Everyone gets nervous. It is completely normal and doesn't mean you are lacking in confidence.

CHAPTER 15:

Celebration

"Celebrate everything; both accomplishments
and defeats, because both are part of the journey.
Give yourself the gift of celebration and you will
make the journey far more enjoyable!"

— Heather Paris

Take time out to celebrate what you have done!
In today's fast world we move from project to
project without taking a break in between to reap the
benefits of completion. We never slow down and take
time to enjoy an ice cream or throw ourselves a party!
I used to be the same way but now I make time to
enjoy what I have worked so hard for. Each August
I host a "Celebrate Life" party. Each year we try to
do something cool and empowering like, break boards
with our hands, or eat fire, or walk on a tightrope.
Participation is voluntary, of course, but the party is
always fun and we have a big cake that says "celebrate

life." These celebrations always include an abundance of food and friends!

We also take time to celebrate things like report cards, art awards, completed projects, or friends and family. Occasionally, we just declare "our family rocks" and throw an impromptu celebration. The celebration doesn't have to be anything formal; it could just be a trip to the ice cream parlor, a yummy dessert after dinner, or even a movie night. Whatever it is you decide to do, let the family know the reason for the occasion is to "CELEBRATE!" Enjoy that time with the family, laugh with them, and have fun. Life is an exciting adventure; we just have to be willing to participate. Don't miss out on the fun. Life waits for no one; either live it or miss it!

You can even celebrate when things don't go your way by celebrating the fact that there must be a bigger picture that you don't see. Celebrate that you woke up and even if things didn't go your way, you have faith that things will ultimately work out. Think about a problem or challenge you had a year ago and celebrate that it is no longer an issue. Whatever it is, just make time to celebrate, be grateful for the journey, and enjoy life!

A life lesson in CELEBRATION:

As I mentioned, every August I have a "Celebrate Life" party. Well the first year I ever had this party, I had big plans! I had tons of awesome food, a huge cake that said "Celebrate Life," lots of friends, family, music and laughing. I even had a happy board; it was a huge display board and a pile of colorful sticky notes. People could write positive affirmations or things they were celebrating on the sticky note and add it to the board. The bright board was full of happiness by the end of the party! I had planned to do a "board break" for the party, to celebrate our strength and to demonstrate how we "break through things that hold us back." I went first, now I had done this before, I was a pro already, so I was going to show everyone how to do it. So I got ready, I stood firm, breathed deep and WACK, I hit the board and it didn't break! I turned and looked at the crowd of about 20 people staring at me and I smiled and stated "See, it's not a trick!" I hit that darn board 4 or 5 more times and it still didn't break and after all that my hand was really sore. I laughed about the strength of that board but got into a ready state again, thought about how I wanted to break through that board and celebrate with my friends, and I focused intensely and broke through it finally! After I did it, everyone else did it too! Even the smaller kids did it by breaking it with their foot and everyone was excited that they were able to break through! I swear that board was oak not pine! But in the end, we all had an amazing time. We even went through the room and each spoke about something we were grateful to celebrate, and then we sang some karaoke. It was a great party and everyone had a wonderful time. My guests thanked me, they said they were reminded that they didn't need an occasion to celebrate and enjoy life. After that, I went and soaked my sore hand and reflected on how much I had to celebrate!

QUICK TIPS:

~ Make time to celebrate when you complete something.

~ Teach your kids/family to celebrate accomplishments.

~ Make a list of all that you are grateful for and refer to it daily.

CHAPTER 16

Growth

"Evolve beyond your circumstances; fancy belongings and an impressive home pale in comparison with your inner spirit."
— Heather Paris

Growth is a process of mature evolution that helps us have a deeper knowledge of and appreciation for life's offerings. I often say, "if you are not growing as a person, you are just slowly dying." Grow your mind by learning new things; take a class, read a book or go to a workshop. You need to evolve and grow in order to feel you are progressing on your journey through life. When you don't pursue growth, you become stagnant and feel as if life is passing you by. If you start to feel "stuck," pick up a personal development book or join a new group or club and meet new people. Sometimes, growing means finding a new group of people to spend your time with. If you grow beyond your circle of friends, you may feel like they are weighing you down. You are the sum of those you associate with so raise your standards and spend time with people who have what you want or who are living the life you would like. It is much better to surround yourself with people that will inspire you than those who will drag you down.

Growth occurs when you let go of what you thought you knew to make room for new concepts and ideas. Take what you like and leave the rest, but always learn and move forward. Life is a journey, not a destination. You never truly arrive, so keep going, keep learning, keep growing and enjoy the ride!

A life lesson in GROWTH:

I haven't stopped growing emotionally or mentally; I am still a work in progress. However, the biggest "growth spurt" that I can remember was many years ago. I often refer to this story as, "The Day I Got off the Couch."

At the time, I was selling real estate, working as the office manager at a design company, running my own rubber stamp company, and caring for my small children as a single parent. I had come home from work one day and, as you might imagine, was exhausted. I knew the kids would be home in about one and a half hours and that gave me just enough time to take a nap on the couch. I had just lay down and gotten comfortable when I remembered I had signed up for a one hour class at my real estate company. I was completely prepared to blow it off and take that nap but I felt too guilty to shirk my commitment to attend. The thought of how I would feel if I offered to do a presentation and no one showed up was enough motivation to get me off the couch. I dragged myself, rather disheveled, to my office and went to the one hour presentation.

That presentation took my journey of personal growth to the next level. The presenter was Jairek Robbins, Anthony Robbins' son, and he gave an inspirational talk about living with passion; I was hooked! I signed up at the end of the presentation to go to a live Anthony Robbins event that was scheduled for later that year: Unleash the Power Within. I went home with a new energy and an excitement about this event in Toronto that I signed up for. I wasn't sure how I was going to get there since I hated to fly...minor detail!

A few months later, I had my passport in hand and boarded the plane for Toronto. I went to the event, I walked on fire for the first time, I made life changing decisions, and I never looked back! Directly after that event, I made a lifetime commitment to vegetarianism, started exercising, kicked my addiction to soda, and started my own women's empowerment company. I quit my job as a real estate agent, I volunteered as a crew member for several Anthony Robbins events, and I even lost 20 pounds after a couple of months of healthy diet and exercise. My life was completely changed. I put all of my efforts into empowering other women and focused on helping single moms. I hosted monthly meetings, attended networking events, and offered free coaching. By this time, I had become a certified coach and started to really grow as a person. I was reading every self help and personal growth book I could get my hands on, I was taking classes and workshops, and networking with other people like me. While expanding my personal horizons, I continued to grow my women's empowerment business and was able to assist thousands of women and children in need. I have since refocused my coaching to include everyone, not just women, and I continue to feed my insatiable desire for knowledge and personal growth. It is difficult for me to imagine myself achieving this level of growth without taking that first step and getting off the couch that day and attending that one hour presentation. I will always be grateful for that seemingly insignificant decision.

QUICK TIPS:

   ~ Read, learn, and take classes or workshops.

   ~ Surround yourself with like-minded people.

   ~ Try new things to discover something new.

CHAPTER 17

Wealth

"You wouldn't wish for a hammer if what you really wanted was
a house. Like the hammer, money is just a tool; focus on what
you actually want and use the proper tools to achieve your goals"
— Heather Paris

oney is not evil, it is awesome! It allows you
to do so many things that you would not
be able to accomplish, otherwise. I would encourage
you all to adopt a different attitude about money if
you think you don't like it or think it is evil. Money is
really nothing more than a tool; something that allows
us to get what we really want. Maybe you want more
time with loved ones, fun toys to enjoy and share, quiet
time with your lover, or even a home to shelter your
family. When you view money in a negative light or
you believe you are unworthy to possess it, you create a
block against it coming into your life. Personally, I love

money and I want to open myself up to receiving lots of it. With money, I can do what I love to do most: GIVE!

Thad and I love to give and help people as much as we can. The more money we get, the more we can do! We also like to enjoy things like eating out, playing with our outdoor toys, and having a nice home to share with our family. We could not do those things if we didn't make money. I would encourage everyone to make friends with wealth and to live in abundance. Remember, when we hold on so tightly to something because we are afraid it will leave us, it will. Living in a state of lack is detrimental to your financial health. Adopt a healthier outlook about money, love it for all that it allows you to do, release it freely knowing you will be taken care of, and teach your kids how to handle money as well.

A life lesson in WEALTH:

I have always loved giving and having enough to give has always been so important to me. Even when I was a struggling single mom, I made sure to give or do what I could to help others. I would often bake things to bring to the elderly and donate my time by volunteering. I once talked my boss into paying for a Christmas party at a homeless shelter. He gave me $1000. and I planned the entire thing! I talked Walmart into giving me a discount on all the toys I bought and I purchased all the food for the party at a wholesale club. There was more than enough food and I had a beautifully wrapped gift, personalized with names on them for every single child at the shelter! I got a co-worker to dress as Santa and I dressed like an elf with a friend. Santa called out each and every child's name and gave the unsuspecting kids each a gift. They were so excited, as I am sure they didn't expect to get anything besides the meal. I also had a couple of teens come and volunteer and they got community service credit for school. The television news crew was there and interviewed me and the shelter workers. It was so awesome and a great way to give back! I truly believe that when you give, you receive. Wealth isn't always about money, being wealthy in goodness and kindness is just as important. The law of reciprocity teaches us that what we give we get. So give freely of your wealth, time, heart and you will receive the same in return!

QUICK TIPS:

~ Money is a tool. Use it as such.

~ Attract money by focusing on what you really want rather than the money.

~ The more money you have, the more you can give!

CHAPTER 18:

Motivation

"Motivation is a byproduct of inspiration. If you
seek motivation, live an inspired life"
— Heather Paris

Motivation is the desire to take actions required to move toward a goal. Inspiration presents itself in the form of creative ideas that make you feel excited. You find motivation when you set a purpose, instead of a goal, and fuel this with inspiration. Purpose is often described as your "calling" in life. It gives you reason to wake up each day. Personally, I know my purpose is to inspire others to live a passion-filled life. I enjoy helping those in need, especially children. When I am fulfilling my purpose, I feel excited and eager to get going. I feel like I am serving a higher purpose and that my work is meaningful. When people set goals, they are working toward something that doesn't have emotion or inspiration behind it. Anyone can make lists of goals, but a life filled with purpose will keep you motivated to move forward.

Goals are important benchmarks, but you must define your purpose before tackling goals in order to visualize your ultimate path. For example, if you are a real estate agent, instead of verbalizing your goal as, "I will sell twenty houses this year and make a bunch of money." Visualize it instead as, "I will help many families enjoy the benefits of home ownership. I will serve my clients and find them homes they will love to raise their families in."

When you have inspiration behind your purpose, you will be more motivated and more likely to achieve success. When you are serving the needs of others and making a contribution, you will always succeed and will be motivated to continue doing it.

A life lesson in MOTIVATION:

When I started my women's empowerment business, I was inspired by the questions I always received from other single moms. The most common of them being, "How do you handle being a single mom with three kids and three jobs?" My reply was always the same: "What else should I do?" I certainly wasn't willing to sit back and cry about my life. Nor did I think I had anything to be upset about. Life was full of challenges but I was happy and didn't feel like I was lacking anything. However, all the questions gave me a desire to teach other women that they could be happy too, despite circumstances. They could be a single parent and still be happy and fulfilled. That is what inspired me to create a group to inspire other women. I was so inspired and dedicated to the process that the motivation just naturally followed. I was excited to get up each day and check my website and user groups to see if any new women had joined. I did massive amounts of reading and educated myself so I could pass along new concepts that would give these women a healthier psychology. I began publicly speaking and the more I did, the more I loved it. These speaking engagements fed my motivation and compelled me to try and help more and more women and kids. Anyone can have that motivation if they find something that will remind them of how good it feels to pursue passion. I often use loud rock music to get me into a state of preparedness and get me pumped up and excited to help others.

It is also important to find your ability level and stick to it. I know what I can afford to do or give and I make sure not to over extend. I never allow myself to feel bad for what I cannot do. I also do daily mantras to remind myself of how good I feel when I am motivated and working toward my purpose and passion. I recite "I am a beacon of love and light and I inspire people!" I also have a note that says "Consistent focus and action!" as a reminder to keep my focus on what I am working towards. Motivation comes from inspired action, give yourself positive reinforcements and reminders and you will be surprised how motivated you become!

QUICK TIPS:

~ Define your inspiration if you want motivation!

~ Discover your true purpose.

~ Recite daily mantras to remind you to stay focused.

CHAPTER 19:

$\mathcal{H}$appiness

*"Happiness is inevitable when you realize you can
choose how to interpret your experiences."*
— Heather Paris

$\mathcal{H}$appiness is an emotional state of joy that comes from a peaceful surrender to all that is and a belief that all things work out exactly as they were intended to. Acknowledge that you have no control over the actions of other people or the outcome of circumstances and happiness is sure to follow.

Energy is contagious. If we project negative energy, so do the people around us. I have heard that people are fifty percent more likely to absorb the energy of what they feel and are surrounded by. So, in theory, we are responsible for what our friends, peers and family feel. Happiness and inspiration are worth spreading!

I have come to realize I am like a tiny pebble being

thrown into a pond. When the pebble hits the water, it creates ripples. Likewise, when people see and hear the things I say and do, they are affected by those words and actions. Every day, I receive e-mails and messages from people who say they were inspired by a particular blog post or things that I have done. Nothing makes me happier than receiving those messages. It makes me remember my purpose and I strive to be an inspiration to others.

We can all do this, as we all have a "circle of influence." You can influence your friends, your family, your neighbors and co-workers, your children and spouses, and even the clerk at the grocery store. If the clerk asks, "How are you today?" Notice how he reacts to your response. Does he look uncomfortably downward or break eye contact? Or, does he light up with a smile and efficiently process your transaction? As you pass energy on to other people, do you want to give them the best of you or would you prefer to give them your worst? Obviously, you should always pass on the best of you.

Every morning when you wake you have a choice to make. You can choose to be happy or to be unhappy. It is never too late to choose to be happy. Happiness is a choice that you must make. The Buddha once said, "Pain is inevitable, suffering is optional." The choice to suffer or not is up to you. Even during the hardest of times in your life, you can choose to see the positives that really can be found in every situation. And even if you don't know what that positive thing may be, at least believe that something positive will come from it.

We all get sad; we all have hard days. However, you don't have to stay with those thoughts or feelings. Today, choose to find the beauty in tough situations. Remember fondly those you have lost. Focus on the positive, be grateful for all you have and think about those who love you. Be kind to everyone but most of all, choose life, choose love, and always choose happiness!

A life lesson in HAPPINESS:

What is worse than not choosing happiness? Being miserable and calling it happiness. For years I let happiness pass me by, I chose to self loathe and, with a smile on my face, claimed to be "fine." I would allow only fleeting moments of happiness in the chaos and drama that I had created for my life. I resigned myself to mediocrity because I was afraid to move forward. I had already made so many mistakes and often thought, "what if I made another?"

I lived my life in fear of judgment and ridicule until, one day I realized that nobody would ever judge or ridicule me more than I had done to myself. I was single-handedly creating my life, my limits, and my unhappiness. I alone had the power to change. I alone had the power to start seeing things clearly instead of through the veil of fear. I alone, should forgive myself for my mistakes.

I had always been a relatively happy person and I wanted that back. I wanted to remove the mask of strength that wasn't really protecting me. I wanted desperately to believe in love again. I wanted to be that kid who protected other kids, and the friend who laughed until it hurt, and most of all, I wanted to be loved. I wanted to feel safe enough to be completely, 100% open and honest and vulnerable with someone. I also wanted that "someone" to love me fully, for all that I am, and all that I am not. I never thought it would happen but it did finally, but only after I healed myself.

This transformation didn't happen overnight; it took some time. I submerged myself in personal development. I read books, I learned to meditate, I started to tell my story, and I figured out what I really wanted in life. Slowly, I increasingly opened up to the people around me. I upgraded my circle of friends and surrounded myself with like-minded, and loving people. I recreated my life to be the way I wanted it and learned to appreciate every moment.

I realized that only I could choose happiness and this was a choice that I wanted to make for the rest of my life. Life has certainly not been perfect or easy since this realization. In fact, sometimes life is painful and difficult! But that is OK, because I know I can handle it, I know it will pass, and I know that happiness never has to leave me, even when times are tough. This happiness is the joy deep within my heart that believes in something much greater than myself. Something that is always working for the greater good, despite how I might perceive it in the moment.

I know now that pretending to be strong, tough, or even indifferent will never shield me from pain. In fact, it is that very pretending that never allows you to open up to every humans true nature which is loving kindness. I know now that pushing people away doesn't keep me from getting hurt, it only prolongs the suffering. I would rather be hurt a million times than feel the ongoing pain and isolation that comes from keeping people out. It is that fear that slowly kills you. It diminishes your spirit, controls your mind, and robs you of precious and limited time. Relationships with other people are the only things that truly matter. The loving connections we make resonate through generations... just ask your grandparents! Had they not met, you would not be here.

Happiness is a choice. I avoided it for a few years and let myself fall into despair and self pity and those were the loneliest years of my life. I slowly pulled myself out, allowed myself to heal, and made peace with the choices I had made. It was then that I started choosing happiness. Happiness was in me all along, I just forgot about it for a while.

People often sit for hours, even days, contemplating the meaning of life. I think it's pretty simple; life is about being happy and being happy is about living inspired, loving fully, and being true to who you are. Choose happiness, and live inspired now!

QUICK TIPS:

~ When feeling down, change your focus. Recall a happy event.

~ Use mantras like, "I am a giver of love and light to all."

~ Remember daily what you are grateful for.

~ Energy is contagious. Spread HAPPINESS!

~ Choose HAPPINESS and... Live Inspired Now!

The End.

BIBLIOGRAPHY

Though most of my ideas come from life experience, I have learned so much from the training I have received as well as the books I have read, and even movies I have watched. Here is a list of the books, movies, and the coach training I have utilized that may have influenced my beliefs and opinions. I recommend them as great tools on your own personal journey!

BOOKS:
Butler-Bowdon Tom - *50 psychology classics: who we are, how we think, what we do : insight and inspiration from 50 key books* - Nicholas Brealey Pub. - 2007

Byrne Rhonda- *The secret* - Atria Books - 2006

Carnegie Dale- *How to win friends and influence people* - Simon and Schuster - 1981

Coloroso Barbara - *Kids are worth it!: giving your child the gift of inner discipline* - W. Morrow - 1994

Dyer Wayne - *The shift: taking your life from ambition to meaning* - Hay House, Inc. - 2010

Edelstein Michael R. - Steele David Ramsay - *Three minute therapy: change your thinking, change your life* - Glenbridge Pub. - 1997

Faulkner Charles - *NLP: the new technology of achievement.* Simon & Schuster - 1996

Frankl Viktor E.- *Man's search for meaning: an introduction to logotherapy* - Beacon Press - 1992

Gray John - *Men are from Mars, women are from Venus: a practical guide for improving communication and getting what you want in your relationships* HarperCollins - 1992

Hill Napoleon - *Think and grow rich* - Melvin Powers, Wilshire Book Co. - 1966

Lama XIV.Dalai - Alexander Norman- *Beyond Religion. ; Ethics for a Whole World.* McClelland & Stewart - 2012

Laozi, Mitchell Stephen- *Tao te ching: a new English version*- Harper & Row - 1988

Markova Dawna - Powell Anne- *How your child is smart: a life changing approach to learning* - Conari Press - 1992

Orloff Judith - *Positive energy: 10 extraordinary prescriptions for transforming fatigue, stress, and fear into vibrance, strength, and love* - Harmony Books - 2004

Robbins Anthony, *Awaken the giant within: how to take immediate control of your mental, emotional, physical & financial destiny*- Summit Books - 1991

Seligman Martin, *Learned Optimism*- A.A. Knopf - 1991

Tolle Eckhart- *The power of now: a guide to spiritual enlightenment*- New World Library - 1999

Wilde Stuart - *The little money Bible: the ten laws of abundance* - Hay House - 2001

Ziglar Zig- *See you at the top* - Pelican Pub. Co. - 1979

MOVIES:

Forks over knives: Monica Beach Media - 2011

Fried green tomatoes - *Universal Pictures* - *1991*

Life is beautiful: "La vita e bella" (original title) - *Buena Vista Home Entertainment* - *1999*

What the bleep do we know!? - 20th Century Fox - 2004

WEBSITES:
The Robbins-Madanes Center for Strategic Intervention
Anthony Robbins, and Cloe Madanes.
www.robbinsmadanestraining.com

Thank you to my friend Michelle Cady who took the cover photo of me. See her work at:
http://www.infinitespirit.biz/